What Readers Are Saying

"St. Augustine testified— "In my deepest wound I saw your glory, and it astounded me." It has been a solemn and stirring privilege to walk with our friends Ian and Gerda through a difficult path they would not have chosen, to witness their transformative discovery of life's greatest treasure—the deep love of Jesus for them."

Richard and Moira Brown

Richard Brown—former COO Working for Orphans and Widows (WOW)

Moira Brown—author, speaker, former co-host 100 Huntley Street

"A genuine Love story that demonstrates true Faith while offering everyone Hope."

Ron Hannah

Past President Promise Keepers Canada

"This is a simple love story – a story that inspires, encourages, and warms. Ian holds high the gift of covenant marriage while acknowledging the unwelcome challenges of life. Ian and Gerda's story is real and relatable. Let it hearten you and yes, even instruct you."

Michael B. Pawelke, DMin
President, Briercrest College and Seminary

"With raw honesty, Ian invites us to bear witness to his story of love, loss and hard-earned lessons. He encourages us towards a personal relationship with Jesus that lights our path when we can't find our way through sadness and grief."

Shirley L Thiessen
Founder, CornerBend Grief Ministries

"This book has inspired me to become better, live better, and love better. The gift of a spouse is something to be cherished deeply, yet too often taken for granted. Yellow A Love Story doesn't allow for such complacency and invites readers to experience a far greater love story—a divine romance between God and oneself. This compelling work draws the reader into an exhilarating, eternal journey of love with the One who created us."

John Friesen
CEO, Muskoka Bible Centre

"A compelling read from the very first page, making it difficult to set aside. The book captivates readers with its portrayal of genuine love, beautifully intertwined with authentic faith that endures through grief and hardship, all within the framework of a grounded, real-life marriage. A truly inspiring tale in a world often marked by brokenness."

Issam Khoury

Bible teacher, translator, and interpreter, ministering alongside his wife Abla to Syrian and Arab communities in Halifax, Nova Scotia.

"Ian and Gerda led lives that were both private and public. Their story unveils a journey filled with love, loss, heartbreak, and hope. I found myself, and my emotions, deeply reflected in much of their experience."

Bud Penner

Former President, Associated Gospel Churches of Canada

"Ian's writing is beautiful and evocative, painting vivid pictures of love and longing both temporal and eternal. Short chapters that make it an easy, enjoyable and rewarding read well worth the investment of time."

Don Moore

Executive Director, Canadian Christian Business Federation

"An amazing story of pursuing love and transformation of the heart through God's love in good times and hard times"

Marcel Knot

E3 Ministry Canada

The Lord speaks to Ian through a colour, but Ian speaks to us of the Lord through his loss. I met Ian while he was still deeply mourning Gerda, but that mourning has turned to dancing. He has become an Apostle to those who have lost the desire of their heart and found the desire of their soul."

Mike O'Leary

Former President, Young Life of Canada

"For anyone who has faced dark valleys in life, this book reminds us that all great love stories are interlaced with the greatest love story of all time; God's loving pursuit of you. As you read this book, you will be drawn into the story of young love, deep pain and devastating loss, and you will find, through it all, a thread of God's love that can be found and pulled through even the darkest of circumstances."

Paul Eastwood

Senior Pastor, Compass Point Bible Church, Burlington.

"I found myself having to take an emotional pause, and realize that for all of us, pain has a joyful purpose. A telling love story that will transform your darkest moments."

Robert Melnichuk

Director, YES TV Western Canada

"Similar to watching a movie, you will be both captivated and transported as Ian passionately reflects on the love and life that he shared with his sweetheart, Gerda."

Linda Joy

Canadian Christian Author of the Journey from Redemption to Restoration and Ministry Moments and Quiet Reflections series.

"Joy, sorrow, laughter, tears … all the ups and downs of a wonderfully narrated love story. So many rich lessons, so much to lift one's spirits, and so much to ponder—especially the Lord's great Love Story with humanity."

Mike and Chris Treneer

Navigators International President Emeritus

"An honest, vulnerable, open-hearted testament to the love of a man and a woman, and also to the overarching love of God who reveals Himself in the midst of the mystery of marriage and the shadows of suffering."

Jill Weber

24-7 Prayer and Waverley Abbey

A heartwarming and poignant love story that is both charming and easy to read. The synchronistic way their paths crossed and the role of their faith in bringing them closer together and sustaining their marriage is truly inspiring. The colour yellow beautifully symbolizes their strength in God. I highly recommend this book to readers of all backgrounds, whether faith-based or not.

Charles Sathmary

Rev Dr. Charles J. Sathmary

"This is much more than a love story. It beautifully highlights Gerda's life and courage while capturing Ian's crushing disappointments and unwavering perseverance. Woven throughout is the hope and comfort of the Lord Jesus Christ. A rich and inspiring read."

Gerry Organ

Former Star Player with The Ottawa Rough Riders

Yellow

a love story

Discovering treasures hidden in dark places

Ian W. McSporran

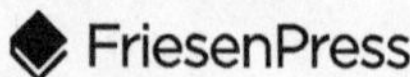

One Printers Way
Altona, MB R0G 0B0
Canada

www.friesenpress.com

First Edition — 2025

ISBN
978-1-03-919159-4 (Hardcover)
978-1-03-835737-3 (Hardcover)
978-1-03-919158-7 (Paperback)
978-1-03-919160-0 (eBook)

1. RELIGION, CHRISTIAN LIVING, LOVE & MARRIAGE

Distributed to the trade by The Ingram Book Company

Contents

PREFACE

Why would I, a lifelong REALTOR® who has never had the slightest desire to write a book, suddenly put pen to paper to write a story, of all things, about love? I wasn't a writer, and had never imagined writing a book, but I knew this story had to be told. Unexpectedly, the task of telling it fell to me. I see now that despite life's challenges, confusions, heartaches, injustices, and unanswered questions, love conquers all.

This is *my* story, or more accurately, *our* story—mine and my wife Gerda's—from my perspective. It tells of the wonder of love we experienced, especially during the last fourteen months of my sweetheart's life.

Thank You!

Initially, I was not going to write acknowledgments because I wanted to keep the book "unburdened" with what I considered traditional book-writing norms, including this one concerning acknowledgements. When my editor challenged my reasoning, I immediately thought, *If I comply, where do I begin?* So many have played such an important part in our lives, and with this book, I feared missing someone, but decided to go ahead and take the risk. If I have forgotten anyone, please forgive me. Let me know for another edition.

My family immediately came to mind. Without them, my last several years would truly have been much lonelier and darker. They walked every step of the way beside me and my dear wife—their mother and grandmother. Since then, they have continued to be a huge support with hugs, tears, prayers, and delicious food! Susan, Liz, David, Jordan, Mandy, Nya, Kyenne, Makayla, Liam, Kyleigh, Julia and Bennett: You were there at every turn, twist, and bump. Thank you, also, Clara and Maelyn for infusing joy into my life in the nine months following your grandmother's passing by joining us in this journey. Jeff, thank you for supporting your family to visit your mother-in-law and me in Germany.

Thank you to three very special friends, Richard and Moira Brown and Debbie Moir-Tigchelaar, who from the first day I spoke about writing the story, have continually whispered words of encouragement and guidance to me. You were invaluable cheerleaders, especially at times when I asked myself: *Who will want to read it?* Debbie, thank you for the countless hours you dedicated to working through my handwritten notes, tweaking and transforming my "chicken scratch" into numerous drafts.

Who knows where I would be without you, my volunteer editors, who helped make this story readable? Richard and Moira Brown, Linda Milke, Don Fletcher, Lorna Dueck, Susan Page, and Serge Proulx: Thank you for not being afraid to slash and cut and for challenging my format. Thank you, also, Aimee

Reid for being the first to do an edit and encouraging me to persevere. I'm so grateful to Eleanor McAlpine for being the final editor, catching errors—including horror of horrors, the misspelling of Gerda's name in one instance.

Aileen Fretz and Reid Lambshead, you were so supportive from the first time I shared the idea of this project with you. You freely gave your artistic skills and always enthusiastically cheered me along. Also Reid, thank you for the precious family photographs you took of me and my family seven weeks before Gerda passed away.

A heartfelt thank you to Nya, my eldest granddaughter, for your exceptional talent in designing the book cover and assisting me with countless computer tasks. Your invaluable contributions were instrumental in bringing this book to completion and publication! Many thanks to Charles Legge for stepping in with technical assistance when Nya was unavailable.

Josh Tiessen, thank you for the masterpiece that adorns the cover of this book. How privileged I am to have an international, award-winning artist link arms with me in this very special way!

To my amazing editor Daina Doucet, who was brave enough to work with me and help me weave this story together, I am so thankful for you. Your insightful questions made me dig hard into the deep recesses of my mind and soul. After our second meeting at Mikel Coffee in Westdale, Hamilton, I could see your incredible gift for editing and knew it would be a blessing to have you guide me in bringing this story to life.

Thank you Francesca at Friesen Press for your very patient guidance in taking me through the publishing process. You were incredibly helpful and informative, making the process as easy and smooth as possible.

Christine at Web Geko, it was an absolute pleasure working with you on the web design. You and your team made the process seamless and delivered such outstanding results.

I feel great love and appreciation toward our extended families, who have been there for us in every season of our lives. On Gerda's side were her widowed mother and her brothers John and David, with their families. Her family, including her father and Oma (grandmother), were very special to her. Gerda treasured those relationships, especially the richness of her conversations with her brothers.

On my side was another indomitable matriarch, my widowed mother, who drilled into me and my siblings that "There is no such word as 'can't' in the English language," meaning there is no excuse for not completing a task you set out to do. My father and mother, along with my siblings Kathy, Neil, Liz, Duncan, and their families, always supported us in many significant ways.

Jessie Cooper, Gerda and I are eternally grateful for your prayerful words of counsel that were filled with truth and healing and played such a pivotal role in our lives.

Friends, friends, friends! Where would we have been without you? You have always been there for us in good times or challenging times like this unique season. You reached out in special ways with cards, notes, meals, help with expenses, phone calls, and visits. A huge thank you to all, including Bud and Beulah Penner, Frank and Nancy Lupton, Susan Page, Cherylene Stimers, Fred and Glenda DeVries, Theresa Vander Laan, Susan Bridle, Ian and Charlotte Kirk, Gerry and Annie LeGault, Esther Abrahams Romanyk, Mark Baker, Beth Hunter, Ray and Yvonne Rhona, Charles Sathmary, Richard and Moira Brown, Jim Fisher, Ron Hannah, John Friesen, Debbie Moir-Tigchelaar, Marcel Knot, Tanya Batagelj, Norah Knox, Vic and Joyce Enns, Steve and Georgie Kearns, Susan Fraser, Lisa Klinck, Becky Armstrong, Jane and George Cordiner, Mary and Arnold Smith, Helen Potocki, Bill and Muriel Heska, Veronica Gilbert, Ron and Neta Wilms, Nancy Wilms, Amy Dempsey, Cyndi and Dan Nicholson, Penny McKenzie, Tenleigh Pearcy, my work families at Bright Realty Team and Keller Williams Edge and Coldwell Banker Burnhill Realty, Paul Eastwood and our church family at Compass Point Bible Church, Sue and Rob Lambshead, Mary and Phil Spencer, and Val Crawford.

A very special thank you to Abi Glugosh, my business partner and dear friend. With selfless dedication, she took full responsibility for our real estate team, giving me the freedom to spend as much time with Gerda as needed. Her generosity allowed me to be fully present during Gerda's illness and begin adjusting to life without her afterwards.

My deepest gratitude goes to my sweetheart, the love of my life, whom I came to cherish with every fibre of my being.

PART I

CHAPTER 1

Gerda, My Sweetheart

"She was so beautiful!" The words burst from my heart when my children showed me a photograph of their mother and me. They came across it while rummaging through family photos in preparation for my sweetheart's celebration of life service due to take place in a few days. The snapshot was taken in the first few months of our marriage as we sat at the dining table enjoying a leisurely breakfast in our housecoats.

I drank in her beauty. So youthful! So absolutely stunning! Her eyes lovingly embracing mine. Tears streamed effortlessly down my face at the recollection, as heartache and grief—deeper than ever before—consumed me. The realization that I would never again gaze into those lovely emerald-green eyes or feel the warmth of her affectionate embrace was almost unbearable.

CHAPTER 2

Our Meeting

I was ready to celebrate. It was summer 1976, and I had just graduated from Estate Management at Southampton College of Technology, now Solent University, in England. My good friend Mark Baker and I were about to embark on a hitch-hiking tour across North America, which included attending the Olympics Games in Montreal, Quebec—a lifelong dream come true. It was my big adventure before starting a job search and settling down in the working world.

When we arrived in Montreal, we found a volunteer hospitality program offering practical support to Olympic attendees. We reached out to the program coordinators to see if they needed additional help. At the operations centre, we were introduced to *Aide Olympique,* which was organised by YWAM (Youth with a Mission). After introducing ourselves and offering our assistance, one of the organisers, perhaps expecting us to decline, said hesitantly, "Well, actually, we are short of help in the kitchen for making meals. Would you be willing to do that?"

Mark answered decisively, "If that's where we're needed, that's where we'll go."

That day, we joined Alfie DeMerchant's culinary team to prepare food each morning in a downtown Montreal church kitchen. By midday, a cafeteria-style, three-course lunch was ready to serve in the church hall for anyone looking for a hearty meal for just a few dollars. We also bagged lunches to sell inexpensively or give away to people on the streets. Our reward was a free lunch—a huge blessing for two "vagabonds" on a very tight budget. It also gave us the chance to connect and share stories with guests and fellow volunteers during meal times.

Working there was such a joy. The atmosphere was vibrant and full of energy, both in the kitchen and the dining room. For an extrovert like me, it was heaven. I was totally in my element making new friends and connecting with people from all over the world.

In this setting, Gerda strolled into my life. How it happened, I have no idea, but there she was suddenly among the group of my new-found friends. She and her friend Marlice were one of the teams that distributed bagged lunches to people in the streets. Afterward they would return to the church to share a meal with everyone.

One day they introduced me to an Australian named Johannes whom they had met during one of their outings.

He enjoyed our pop-up restaurant and, over the next few days, became a regular. We looked out for each other and had many engaging conversations about our interests and other things in life.

One day, as we sat eating, Johannes leaned toward me and whispered, "She's a beautiful girl." A bit startled by his out-of-context statement, I asked, "Who are you talking about?"

"You know, Gerda."

"Oh! Gerda? Yes," I replied hesitantly, thinking, *Hmm! Next time I see her, I'll have to take a closer look.*

That's exactly what I did later that day, and when I saw her, my heart leapt! *My goodness! He's right,* I thought. Over the next three days, without trying to make my interest in her too obvious—at least so I believed—I spent as much time as I could around her. Whether it was in the restaurant, shopping, exploring the streets of Montreal, going for ice cream or attending YWAM rallies, I found every excuse to be near her.

The more time I spent with her, the more intrigued I became by her depth of character and the captivating aura she carried. Outwardly she was stunning—slender and graceful at five feet, six inches, with shoulder-length brown hair and sparkling green eyes. But her beauty went far beyond appearances. I saw a very loving person with a quiet, gentle spirit and profound passion for exploring life's biggest questions. I felt a strong pull towards her and was certain she was someone I wanted to keep in contact with afterward.

When our time together in Montreal was winding down, I was thrilled Gerda invited Mark and me, "should your travel permit," to visit her at her parents' home in Niagara-on-the-Lake, close to Niagara Falls.

Of course, our travels would permit! Without a moment's hesitation, the visit was on our itinerary.

Mark and I left Montreal in style with one of our new friends, Barb Hyde, in her father's twenty-nine-foot luxury motor home. We stretched out in the back of this hotel on wheels while Barb's father drove us to Toronto. From there, we continued our adventure, visiting as many famous tourist sites in the United States as possible, spectacular places like Mount Rushmore, the Badlands of South Dakota, Yellowstone National Park with its amazing wildlife and the Old Faithful geyser, and our ultimate destination, San Francisco. There we split up, since Mark was flying back to England before me.

CHAPTER 3

Special Attraction

Four days after Mark left, I set out on the 2,600-mile trek back to Toronto. I was determined to get there as fast as possible to allocate maximum time for a special attraction near Niagara Falls. Through a newspaper advertisement, I found a young man with a car who was in a hurry to get to Ohio, and was looking for someone to share the driving and gas expense. I was thrilled to be chosen, so for the next 32 hours, we drove, stopping only for food, bathroom breaks, refuelling, and driver changes. Any sleeping we did was on the back seat while the other drove.

From Ohio I hitch-hiked again. The moment I got into Canada, I called Gerda. She immediately came to pick me up, welcoming me with a warm hug. I felt a rush of the same closeness I had experienced in Montreal and thought to myself, *So far so good!*

Gerda took me to her parents' ten-acre fruit farm on the edge of picturesque Niagara-on-the-Lake. Over the next three days, she and her family hosted me with exceptional hospitality.

As planned, Mark had already gone by to see Gerda. Apparently he was one of a number of young men who had already visited her after the Montreal Olympics. I had some stiff competition.

I had a wonderful time with Gerda, her family, and good friend Annie who came along to attractions like Fort George, Niagara Falls and Marineland.

Fort George, with its twelve-foot wooden-stake defensive walls, had been a key military outpost during the Canadian/American war in the early 1800's. On our way by, Gerda proudly pointed it out to me. In my mind I chuckled to myself thinking, *You call that a FORT! It's walls are like matchsticks. You should see Lancaster Castle!* In high school, I walked by this massive fortress everday—its towering sixty-six-foot-high stone walls, ten feet thick, were a sight to behold.

The world-renowned Niagara Falls waterfalls, however, left me with the opposite impression to Fort George. It was exhilarating to stand at the edge of the thundering water cascading just below our feet into a bottomless pit obscured by mist.

How is it possible for so much water to run over the edge and for the river upstream never to run dry? I wondered.

One day we went for afternoon tea in Niagara-on-the-Lake at an English tea shop. Gerda and Annie were curious to know if it was up to British standards. I assured them it was—as if I knew. During this time together, I cherished the fact that I didn't have to compete for her attention, unlike when we were at the Olympics with other male friends. It allowed me get to know this beautiful young woman on a deeper level. Initially, as we had walked the cobblestone streets of Old Montreal and talked about our families and ancestries, she had shared that she was from a Mennonite family.

Who on earth are Mennonites, I wondered.

My time with her in Niagara-on-the-Lake further deepened my understanding of her heritage. She explained how her ancestors had been invited by Catherine the Great in the late 1700s to move from Holland and South Germany to the Ukraine region of Russia. They were skilled farmers, and their expertise in cultivating the rich, fertile lands were greatly valued and in high demand.

As a result, Gerda's parents were born in Ukraine in the 1920s. It was horrifying to hear of the suffering they had experienced. They lost their land to Stalin's totalitarian policies, and many of their family and friends were tragically ripped from their midst and shipped like cattle to Siberian work camps, never to return. This tragic fate befell one of her grandfathers, two uncles, and other relatives. Her other grandfather, however, was unjustly executed before he could embark on the same journey.

During World War II, Germany attacked Russia, and their soldiers marched through Gerda's parents' home region leaving a trail of destruction. Her dad, fifteen at the time, was given the choice of joining the German army or digging his own grave before being shot. He didn't want to die, so, as a pacifist by faith, when compelled into combat, he defiantly fired his machine gun into the air to avoid taking anyone's life.

Gerda's great grandmother, grandmother, and mom escaped in November 1943 with 35,000 others on "The Great Trek," an arduous twelve-hundred-mile journey by horse and wagon. Sadly only twelve thousand people made it safely to the west with the rest dying on the perilous journey, or being captured and returned to the Soviet Union, often to labour camps, as happened to Gerda's aunt. Eventually both her parents, following divergent paths to freedom, arrived in Canada.

David and Helen Schellenberg met and married in 1950 in St. Catharines, Ontario. They lived on their farm that they worked during their spare time after their day jobs. It was a joy meeting them. The farm interested me, but not as much as my walks with Gerda, during which time she educated me on the varieties of fruit trees and other farming aspects.

A handful of ducks and geese wandered the farm. Their German shepherd, thankfully, was caged. He indicated with his teeth that he would have been happy to have a piece of me.

Her father's pride and joy were his prize-winning homing pigeons, which he raced on weekends from late spring to fall. When their flying days ended, to Gerda's dismay, they became Sunday dinner along with the ducks and geese. She insisted none end up on her plate.

The four days with Gerda were the most wonderful of my whole trip. I ate three meals a day, slept in a comfortable bed, and discovered a new part of the world. Most importantly, I spent time with this beautiful, engaging young woman whom I had come to deeply cherish. She had a way of drawing me in with her loving warmth and charm, making every moment with her feel effortless and meaningful. The more I got to know her, the more I realized how special she was—someone who brought joy and depth into my life in a way I hadn't experienced before.

Far too soon, it was time to leave. Gerda's parents graciously provided me with a bus ticket to Toronto Airport. I dismissed the fleeting suspicion that they were politely making sure this long-haired British hippie didn't miss his flight home. Perhaps, in their own way, they were discouraging a presence that might otherwise persist.

It was a tedious yet contemplative journey home. I was totally smitten with Gerda, and all I could do was think and dream of a future with her. I started writing her a letter to see if she felt the same toward me.

CHAPTER 4

Beached

Back in England I spent the next four days crafting a rambling twenty-four-page letter. I gave Gerda a full report of my flight home and the horrendously long nineteen-hour hitchhiking experience from London to Morecambe, Lancashire, which normally took six to eight hours.

I trekked through many topics, like the bad drought in England and my plans for finding a job, until eventually I bared my soul and expressed the deep affection I felt for her, more than I had ever felt for any girl. I let her know I assumed she had similar feelings toward me and encouraged her to respond with the same openness and honesty we had shared in Canada.

Several weeks passed before I received a response, but it seemed like an excruciatingly long time. I tore open the letter with great anticipation and discovered a card with a round, cartoonish man standing on the circumference of

Earth holding his hands in front of him, wishfully staring off at the stars and moon.

A caption on the front read, "Every time I think of you . . ." and inside the card it read ". . . ZAP! Instant sunshine!" On it was a drawing of a happy-faced sun and the little cartoon man doing a joyful backflip over it. Gerda wrote, "When I saw this card, I thought of you and couldn't resist sending it."

My heart leapt for joy! The card convinced me that we shared romantic feelings for each other.

Eagerly, I delved into her letter, fully expecting to see a written confirmation of her passionate love for me. She wrote exactly like I had asked: "openly and honestly, with no sugar-coating."

"To be honest Ian, I had no idea how you felt. What you said in your letter came as a total surprise to me. Ever since we met in Montréal, I have seen you as a special friend that God has given me. But I saw you only as a friend."

That was it. To the point. Absolutely the last thing I wanted to hear.

A window in the heavens seemed to open and dump an icy deluge on my dreams of a life with Gerda, but I noticed a sliver of silver lining on the edge of that dark cloud: She valued my friendship!

I sighed and put the letter down. At least I was keeping her as a friend. As this reality set in, I started grappling with my lovesickness, wondering if I would ever find someone else for whom I would feel as strongly.

We floundered along for the next eighteen months with intermittent letters. Now and then we commented on how wonderful it would be to sit face-to-face for a good heart-to-heart talk like we had enjoyed during the summer of 1976. And, then, something happened to restore life to our beached relationship.

CHAPTER 5

Reunion

At the end of February 1978, Gerda wrote to say that she and her friend Beth had booked flights to London for the beginning of July. They planned to spend six weeks travelling Europe and hoped to include a few days with Mark and me in Southampton. I protested at the mention of "a few days" and was thrilled to receive another letter in May saying they would extend their time with us. They were not sure for how long, but it would be more than initially planned.

The closer the time came to our reunion, the more excited I got about becoming more than friends. In my classic, impetuous manner, I decided I wanted to find out by the end of our time together if we could move into a romantic relationship, or if I should move on in my search for the right one. I shared these thoughts with a few close friends and asked them to agree with me in prayer for God's direction.

When Gerda and Beth finally arrived, we had a wonderful, fun-filled week, especially with Mark and Beth being as good a comedy duo as you would find anywhere. With their contrasting humour and personalities continually bouncing off one another, we were often doubled over with laughter.

We showed Gerda and Beth as many of the local places of interest as possible. They marvelled at Winchester Cathedral, which had been built across five centuries, beginning in 1079. They were captivated by its Gothic architecture, the seventy-eight-foot-high nave and the psychedelic colours of the stained-glass windows.

Afterward, we swept them off their feet with a fine outdoor dining experience we arranged, thanks to the local take-out "chippy." We treated them to classic English fish and chips wrapped in newspaper and topped with a rose that I had stealthily snitched from someone's front garden. We enjoyed the feast on a park bench.

A few days later, Mark and I treated them to a more elegant experience of afternoon cream tea with white tablecloths, fine china, and silverware at a historic Tudor home in the New Forest National Park, where wild ponies still roam.

Another evening we took them on a mystery excursion—a private and exclusive tour of a Brazilian frigate that Vickers, the shipbuilding company for which Mark worked as an engineer, had just completed. Mark had access to areas that were out of bounds to others. Gerda and Beth were in stitches, laughing as they climbed up and down the ship's many ladders in tight skirts and totally inappropriate footwear. Thankfully, they "took it in good stride" and weren't upset that we hadn't warned them about the nature of our excursion.

Toward the end of our time together, Mark and I were ushers at our friends' wedding in Piddletrenthide, Dorset. Rob and Jackie had kindly invited Gerda and Beth to accompany us. As we approached our destination, the girls began noticing directional road signs that they started reading out loud.

"Piddlehinton!"

"Puddletown!"

"Poundbury!"

"Piddletrenthide on the River Piddle!"

"It's so…so British!" exclaimed Beth, both of them unable to contain explosive bursts of laughter.

The girls were in awe of the historic, austere, and fortress-like stone structure of All Saints Church where the wedding was held. It dated back to the twelfth century, a sight they had not seen in Canada, where buildings are not much older than 150 years.

As we entered the church, I read a sign attached to the front door that gave us a chuckle: "Please close doors to keep out birds (the feathered type)." I could see they didn't understand the dry English humour hidden in this notice. "Bird," I explained, "in England is slang for a young woman, or girlfriend."

For some reason, at this celebration I realised like never before the seriousness of marriage. I have no idea what triggered the thought, but suddenly I just couldn't see myself ready to take that step. Was it fear? I didn't think so, but I had a strong sense that it wasn't the time yet for me to be married. In my "infinite wisdom" I answered the question I had posed for myself: NO! I would not be moving forward in my relationship with Gerda.

On our final night together I invited Gerda to The Bassett, an elegant, local Southampton restaurant. We were shown to our table, which was set in a bay window, tucked quietly away to the side. In my mind, it was a perfect setting to share with this radiantly beautiful woman and enjoy what Gerda later described as "a very romantic candlelit dinner."

During the evening, I explained that I had given a lot of thought to our relationship and believed there was nothing more to it than the friendship we already enjoyed. Looking back, it was an odd thing to do, considering we had not spoken of it since she rejected my advances two years prior.

Gerda listened quietly. Her demeanour didn't change. She expressed no hint of thinking more positively toward me than she had previously, and I didn't ask for her thoughts. Had I asked, I would have learned of her change of heart, something she kept to herself till a number of years later.

The following day Mark and I drove the girls to a local ferry for them to continue their European vacation in France. We accompanied them to the departure gate with

Mark and Beth walking well ahead of us and Gerda slightly ahead of me. I reached toward Gerda and laid my hand on her shoulder. She instinctively wheeled around toward me, and we gave each other a heartfelt, loving hug.

"You will always be one of my very special friends," I told her, "and I will be jealous of anyone you marry."

To this day I still feel the warmth and comfort of that sweet embrace. It seemed so right, as if we belonged in each other's arms. This memory, burning deep inside me, was one of the reasons I knew I had to see Gerda the following year. I really needed to be certain that there was nothing more to our relationship than what we already had.

[illegible] and Rete walking [illegible] and Gerdi [illegible] ahead of me. I reached forward and laid my hand on her shoulder. She turned her wheelchair [illegible] toward me, and we gave each other a heartfelt hug [illegible]

"You will always be one of my very special friends," [illegible] and I [illegible] of my [illegible] heart."

To this day I still feel the warmth and comfort of that sweet embrace. It [illegible] each other [illegible] the moment [illegible] one of the reasons I know I had [illegible] the [illegible] that there was no [illegible] more [illegible] relationship than what we already had.

CHAPTER 6

Candid Words

In the months following Gerda's visit to Southampton, my emotions again became confused. My question about whether she was the right one had been answered, or so I thought, but something kept stirring in me. I found myself asking once again: *Can we be more than friends?* I loved sharing thoughts and feelings in letters with her and started longing to see her. I had to identify the real nature of our relationship.

In the late spring of 1979, I decided to quit my job as an estate agent (British REALTOR®) and change careers to something involving agriculture. I had been raised on a dairy farm and it had always been my desire to have a farming-related career. Being an estate agent wasn't giving me that opportunity. More importantly, this decision gave me a chance to travel to North America to see Gerda, albeit under the guise of visiting friends and family.

I flew into Detroit near my sister Kathy and brother-in-law Kermit's home in Ann Arbor, Michigan, only four hours from Burlington, Ontario, where Gerda now lived. Not knowing her summer plans, I called her as soon as possible after landing to see if she was in town.

She answered, "Oh, my goodness! You are where? What are you doing there?" She was completely surprised to hear my voice.

"Just visiting my sister," I said, grinning broadly, and added, "I thought I might pop by and see you too, if that's okay. I'm only four hours away."

"Oh, yes, of course!" she exclaimed, sounding delighted. "I'd love to see you. Absolutely come and visit me."

I wasn't reading too much into this warm welcome, remembering all too well a similar one three years earlier when I visited her in Niagara-on-the-Lake, after which she made it clear she only saw me as a friend.

A few days later, excited and uncertain of what lay ahead, I crossed into Canada. I knew she had broken up with a boyfriend in March, but didn't know if someone else had already scooped her up. If that were the case, my visit would be short and courteous.

Gerda had just started her summer holidays, and the day I arrived, she and her friend Beth were moving into a new apartment.

As I pulled into the parking lot of her building and got out of the car, she spotted me, shouted "It's Ian!" and ran twenty yards toward me, flinging herself into my arms, saying. "It's so wonderful to see you! I'm so glad you're here!"

Just like in the movies, I thought. Incredulous, happy and surprised, I took it in. It was as though we were long lost lovers, not just good friends. I was astounded by her out-of-character exuberance, so unlike Gerda who never liked drawing attention to herself.

She cheerfully introduced me to those helping with the move, some of whom had just witnessed our passionate reunion. It was wonderful to see Beth's familiar face among the helpers. I listened intently as she presented me to the four young men in her group.

I thought, *if she has a boyfriend, surely he'd be here helping her*, but she didn't introduce anyone as her "boyfriend." From what I saw, she seemed to regard them all as friends. I took it as my green light to go ahead with my real mission without delay.

As we finished the move, Beth informed me that her parents had invited me to stay with them while I was in town. Before heading there for the night, I invited Gerda for a walk. We strolled to Spencer Smith Park which was near her new apartment, offering a peaceful spot by Lake Ontario to enjoy the evening.

As we sat down at a picnic table, catching up on family and friends, I seized the moment and shared what was on my heart.

"I came to see if there might be more to our relationship than just friendship," I said. "Last summer, I thought I had my answer, that we were just meant to be friends. But lately, I've found myself questioning that decision. More and more, I find myself wanting to share with you what's going on in my life. So, I've come to see if there's any chance we can have a future together."

Gerda sat quietly, processing what I had just said without moving, or saying a word. It felt like an eternity, though likely only was just a few moments. Finally she spoke, her voice soft and sincere: "I don't really know what to say, except you are a very special friend who I deeply value and respect. I feel conflicted, too, but I'm not sure how to explain it."

I received these words with a mixture of relief and rejoicing, especially since the last time I had posed this question I received a resounding no.

This puts me way ahead of where I was three years ago, I thought. That night I went to bed "over the moon" with excitement. I was doing back flips in my heart, just like the little cartoon man on Gerda's card she sent me the first time I asked this question. I now held something precious: the *possibility* of spending the rest of my life with this beautiful woman.

During the subsequent two weeks we shared our hearts and feelings toward one another openly and enjoyed our time together hiking in places like Webster Falls, walking the shoreline of Lake Ontario, and visiting her family in

Niagara-on-the-Lake. Both of us recognised more might be possible, but what would it look like? How would it work with us living on different continents? Gerda was very cautious and nervous about long-distance relationships. Having experienced the challenges of one previously, she wasn't eager to jump into another one.

We agreed to take time apart to reflect and pray about the future of our relationship, while I spent two weeks visiting friends in Wisconsin and Alberta. Upon my return, we planned to meet at my sister's house in Ann Arbor to discuss things further.

During our time apart, I took a moment to list all the positives and negatives of our relationship. Once I had everything written down, it became crystal clear to me: Gerda was the one for me.

Then I must be the right one for her too, I reasoned.

Many things played into this revelation, among them, that we brought the best out in each other, including mutual encouragement to grow closer to God, and that after three years, we were both still available. Also, time had allowed us to develop a genuine, respectful friendship and love for one another, a good foundation for any marriage. The only challenge I could see was that we lived on different continents. Considering what was at stake, it seemed totally insignificant to me.

Our first day back together in Ann Arbor was warm and sunny—perfect for a picnic. We found a park with a grand willow tree, spread out a blanket beneath its shade, and savoured our meal while soaking in the beautiful summer weather. I enthusiastically shared the list of reasons why I believed we belonged together, expecting her full agreement considering my sound logic. That wasn't the case. Gerda continued expressing uncertainty. Thankfully she was prepared to continue moving forward in *exploring* the possibility.

With a plan for me to immigrate to Canada, we decided to see if I could find a job around Burlington, but she had a concern.

"What happens if our relationship doesn't work out and you've uprooted yourself from your home and family? You'll be in a foreign country! What if it doesn't work?"

"That's no problem," I replied, thinking to myself, "*This is the adventure of my life, and wild horses can't stop me from coming. Anyway, I know you'll marry me.*"

I had come to appreciate this young woman so deeply. I loved her nature and desire to know God so deeply. Curiosity gave her the insight to ask thoughtful, penetrating questions, and caution didn't allow her to accept simple or evasive answers. Such a contrast to myself! I liked to keep things simple and avoid excessive detail. If someone's point made sense and it worked, that was perfectly fine with me.

A few days later, we headed for Niagara-on-the-Lake. I was booked to fly back to England in five days, so we started to look earnestly for work I could do. Since I had planned to focus on agriculture, we checked out several farm opportunities. A break came a few days later when we saw a small ad in the *Globe and Mail* for a farm worker. My application was a success, and I was offered a job at a dairy farm in Queensville, near Newmarket, an hour-and-a-half from Burlington. We were thrilled. It resonated with both of us. I would have my farming opportunity, and Gerda wouldn't have to deal with an overseas relationship. We didn't anticipate any obstacles.

It would be an understatement to say that returning to Canada didn't go as smoothly as we expected. The farmer's request for my work permit was refused by someone who arbitrarily decided he already had his quota of immigrant workers.

I also applied to the Canadian Consulate in England to emigrate thinking, *It's a slam dunk. I have a job offer, a clean police record, and when they see what a nice guy I am, they'll welcome me to their country with open arms.*

Not exactly!

They weren't impressed with my amazing cow-milking skills and declined my application without explanation. I was totally devastated and broke down in tears when I received the news.

Ironically, our courtship now qualified as an "overseas relationship"—a situation that surprisingly didn't disturb Gerda. It provided her with more time to contemplate our relationship, and allowed me the opportunity to sort out aspects of my life I hadn't realised needed attention.

Before I was denied entry to Canada, I had been experiencing blinding headaches—and the rejection had only exacerbated them. With my return there blocked, and the needs in my life mounting, I sought God, seeking his help.

Shortly after, while I was reading Hebrews twelve, a passage suddenly stood out to me. It said that God disciplines us out of love, just like a father would his child. A thought occurred to me: *Could the headaches be God's way of getting my attention?* I told him, *If these headaches are your discipline in my life, I accept that. Show me where I am wrong.*

Within days the floodgates opened, and suddenly I became aware of many ways I had wronged various people throughout the years. I knew I had to make wrongs right. I had to connect with them.

I reached out to some with letters and spoke to others asking for forgiveness. Some accepted, while others, particularly those I contacted by letter, didn't. The most difficult conversation I had was with my parents, against whom I realized I harboured bitterness and resentment. When I apologised and asked for their forgiveness, my father remained silent, but my mother was visibly hurt by my confession and erupted into an angry outburst, deflecting blame onto someone else for my transgression. Through tears, all I managed to say was, "No! I take full responsibility for my negative feelings toward you." After that there was no further discussion. The topic was never revisited. I believe this moment marked a turning point for the better in our relationship, particularly in my heart.

While seeking forgiveness was challenging, it brought me a sense of inner peace that is difficult to explain. Another surprising, but very welcome outcome was a noticeable and significant decrease in headaches.

Prior to taking this path of reconciliation, I had visited my doctor for help with the headaches. He had arranged a specialist's appointment, but by the time it rolled around, I was convinced it would be a waste of time. I knew the root, but wanted to make sure nothing else was contributing to the problem. Based on a series of tests, the specialist confirmed I was in good health.

My inability to emigrate to Canada was a dark time in my life, but through it I learned some valuable lessons. Specifically, I wrestled with God why I couldn't be with Gerda in Canada. Eventually I accepted that if God was at the centre of our relationship, then he would work out how I would get to be with her. To walk in faith and believe that God would intervene for me in this manner was incredibly challenging, but I knew it was the right way forward. Also in truth, it was the only way.

The delay in getting back to Canada included some additional blessings. That Christmas Gerda arranged to visit me and meet my family in Forton near Lancaster where I was living with my parents.

During our time together we visited several farming friends in the area. I reminisced about my childhood, and how, for the first fifteen years of my life, I had been immersed in farm life seven days a week along with my parents and siblings Kathy, Neil, and Liz.

By four years of age I was gainfully engaged in helping my mother deliver milk to homes in towns and villages near our farm. At thirteen, when my brother Neil was fifteen, our dairy farming skills were so developed that our parents entrusted us to operate the farm by ourselves while they took a well-deserved week's vacation, probably the first since their honeymoon.

Hard work was as normal for me and my siblings as play was for many others, and none of us have ever regretted the work ethic instilled in us as children.

Cuddled in front of a roaring, coal-burning fireplace in my parents' living room, Gerda and I talked about such things daily, often into the early hours of the morning. I pointed out that with the birth of Duncan, my youngest brother, when I was fourteen, I became "piggy in the middle" with an older brother and sister and a younger brother and sister. This placement could have affected my personality, but I didn't notice. I characterise myself as a quiet and inquisitive child, although my siblings might have called me a troublemaker. I must admit, I did cause my family considerable and undue stress. I shared some of the stories with Gerda, but after that

I could almost discern her thoughts: *Am I safe being around this person?*

Several hare-brained schemes stood out, underscoring my inquisitive nature, but I only remember one clearly. By the time I was five, I had drunk turpentine, poked my mother's hatpin into an electrical outlet, and placed my left hand in the wringers of a washing machine. Apparently, my stomach was pumped to remove the turpentine, and the hatpin experiment threw me across the room against the far wall. The washing machine incident, though, I remember clearly.

I was with my mother who was doing the laundry. She left the room momentarily, and I realised this was my opportunity to check out the mechanics of the wringer washer. I pushed a chair up to it, climbed up, and quickly reached for the knob that started the rollers turning. Knowing my mother could return at any moment and interrupt my experiment, I put my left hand into the rollers so I could feel how smooth they were—definitely not one of my smartest ideas.

The pain was excruciating, not just in that moment, but also during the subsequent surgeries and treatments to save my hand from being amputated. Thankfully, the doctors successfully saved it, leaving me with a scarred palm and a little finger substantially longer than my other one. Even today people wince when they see it and hear that story.

While Gerda and I were together, we also visited the seaside town of Morecambe, only twenty minutes from Forton, where my family moved in 1969 after we left the farm. We walked together along the promenade, and I proudly pointed out the stunning views of the mountains across Morecambe Bay in the Lake District, a UNESCO World Heritage Site. I showed her the seven-bedroom guest house we bought when my parents entered the hospitality business, and the eighteen-bedroom hotel we took over a few years later. My mother effectively operated these businesses, and just like on the farm, the children were all expected to work in the family enterprise.

In many ways, the work at Morecambe was a breeze compared to the rigorous farm life of my childhood. As we walked, I recalled how I had honed many important life skills there: house cleaning, bed making, bartending, serving tables, food purchasing, preparation, and presentation, among others. Hotel work was significantly more advantageous due to its seasonal nature and the comfort of remaining indoors during inclement weather. Tips, especially at the bar, were a great help.

Dad worked alongside my mother in the lodging business, but he also had various other jobs before he found his perfect niche selling livestock feed to farmers. This allowed him to talk at great length to his clients about farming and issues of the day—definitely his "sweet spot" regarding work. A farmer once commented that one day Dad arrived in time to sit down for lunch with them and was still there at dinnertime.

When my parents were in their fifties, they sold the hotel and started Bay Travel that specialised in farm tourism. This business still thrives today in Morecambe under the expertise of my brother Neil and his wife Janet. Until the COVID lockdowns in 2020, my mother popped in regularly to check up on everyone and often booked her next travel excursion.

Gerda asked to hear more about my parents' background one evening as we sat by the coal fire. I shared their life stories.

My parents, Angus and Betty McSporran, like Gerda's, had experienced firsthand the horrors of World War II. Dad, first a sailor in the Royal Navy, and then a soldier with the First Battalion of the Seaforth Highlanders, experienced the bloody carnage of war. Many of his friends fell at his side, especially on Omaha Beach during the Normandy landings as part of the Royal Navy Commando unit supporting the U.S. Army.

Mum's teenage years were overshadowed by the war. She spent much of her time bunkered down in her parents' air raid shelter on their farm at Chequerbent whenever nearby Manchester was being bombed. She and my father met and married after the war in 1949 and became hard-working dairy farmers at Foulridge, on the border of Lancashire and Yorkshire, before moving to Barnoldswick.

During the Christmas celebrations, my family and Gerda got to know each other. Gerda was captivated by my mother's culinary skills, even though the kitchen appeared to her as being in complete chaos compared to the neat and orderly system she was used to in her own family's kitchen. She was shocked at the size of the thirty-pound turkey Mum had prepped for Christmas dinner.

"I've never seen one that big!" she exclaimed, and asked me, "How on earth is she going to squeeze it into the oven?"

Sure enough, Mum, who always found a way through a challenging situation, coerced it into the oven, and provided a delicious Christmas dinner with roast potatoes, Brussels sprouts, carrots, stuffing, and gravy to accompany the wonderfully succulent turkey. She finished the meal with mince pies and her delectable trifle soaked in copious amounts of sherry and topped with a thick layer of real whipped cream.

My family was not one to share thoughts or feelings, but toward the end of Gerda's time with us, I asked my parents, "Will you support Gerda and me if we get married? I'm not sure when that'll be, or how it'll all work together, but I wanted to ask you before I ask her to marry me."

Instantly my mother said, "Yes, absolutely. There is always a way to make things work out." For my mother to be so affirmative, without a moment's hesitation, indicated Gerda had won a special place in her heart.

What a Hallmark Christmas movie-style holiday! We spent every waking moment enjoying each other's presence, and the company of my family and friends. Throughout it all, I was secretly planning the perfect moment to ask, "Will you marry me?"

CHAPTER 7

Will You Marry Me?

After Christmas, we stayed with my good friends Ray and Yvonne Rhona in Southampton to celebrate New Year's Eve 1980 with them and other friends, including Mark.

Just past midnight, steeped in joy and anticipation of a good year, I pulled Gerda aside and asked her to marry me. She was dumbfounded and entirely caught off guard.

Not at all having anticipated the question, she absorbed my words wide-eyed, barely whispering, "I don't know. I have to think about it because when I make this decision, I want it to be the right one."

No problem, I thought to myself. *I'm sure she'll have a yes for me after a good night's sleep and time to process it.*

The next morning, Gerda was set to return to Canada.

After saying our goodbyes to Ray and Yvonne, I began the drive to Heathrow Airport in London. Not long into the journey, I turned to her and asked, "So what's your decision?"

Surely, she has had plenty of time to decide to say Yes, I thought confidently as I prepared myself for her answer. After a few moments, to my surprise, she repeated the same uncertain, torn words from the previous evening: "I don't know. If and when I say yes, I want to know for sure it's the right choice."

Once again, I had been charging full steam ahead, only for her words to bring my train to a sudden, jarring halt. My enthusiasm drained away. Still, I cautiously pressed forward, holding onto the hope that she might still say yes before the journey's end.

"You know, I talked to both our parents. They are supportive of us getting engaged..." I began, when her reaction derailed me.

"You did what?" she was aghast. "You called my parents to ask if you could marry me?"

I felt startled and thought, wasn't that the right thing to ask them?

"Yes! Your Dad didn't even hesitate. He said I could marry you. I asked if he wanted to discuss it with your mom, and he said they had already talked about it. They approve of us getting married."

I sensed a cloud of confusion and frustration descending over Gerda.

"Now I have to explain why I'm going back without a ring." I could almost hear her thinking: *How could you do that without me knowing?*

An uncomfortable silence descended in the car as we both retreated into icy coldness. This wasn't going at all like I hoped, and worse, Gerda now was distressed at me for pressuring her to accept. Obviously, I wasn't going to get the answer I desperately wanted.

After what seemed like an eternity, but was probably only two or three minutes, I broke the silence and said somewhat reluctantly, "Take whatever time you need. I don't want you to feel pressured if you are not totally sure yet." I was determined not to part with tension between us, especially after we had had such a wonderful time together.

Not knowing when we would see each other again, we gave each other a long, loving hug at the airport. We prayed for God's protection over our time apart, for his continued blessings, and especially that we might soon be together in Canada.

On my way home I reflected on our time together. I really felt thankful that even though we weren't engaged, our relationship still had potential.

I just have to be patient, I told myself. Patience wasn't my virtue.

We continued our long-distance relationship with letters back and forth and interspersed them with the occasional phone call. That January I received nine letters from Gerda with clear indications that she missed being with me.

She wrote, "I am certainly feeling very positive about our relationship. Please be patient with me. I love you." They were words of sweetness to my soul that affirmed to me my prospects with Gerda were still very much alive.

Then suddenly, at the end of March, our routine was interrupted when Gerda called in excitement to say, "Mr. Cowieson [the farmer] called me. He said he has persuaded the local employment office to give you a work permit, so you are coming to Canada! I can't wait to see you again."

I was shocked and elated at the same time. There had been no indication the chance to move to Canada would materialise.

Within twelve days I had given notice at my temporary job, packed my bags, said goodbye to family and friends, and was on my way again.

It only took me a week in Canada to realise my life savings of four hundred dollars wouldn't go very far toward the price of even the cheapest engagement ring. I would have to save my pennies until I could budget a reasonable amount for it.

In my typical mischievous way, just to get a reaction from Gerda, I said, "I am sorry. I have to withdraw my marriage proposal." Seeing her shock and bewilderment was priceless, but I didn't want her to suffer too long, or think I was no longer committed to her. I quickly explained my financial situation. I wanted her to know without a doubt that I was still seeking a yes from her concerning marriage.

She immediately relaxed and smiled. "Oh! That's okay with me." She agreed with my reasoning, especially because it lifted the pressure off her to make a decision.

Three months later, in July, it was Gerda's birthday. By then I had saved enough money to buy a small ring. My mind raced ahead again. Where would I propose this time?

We had planned to be in Niagara-on-the-Lake that weekend. That would be the place—the perfect, romantic setting. A big improvement from a corner of a room in Ray and Yvonne's house!

I envisioned the spot where I would once again pose the question: the Queens Royal Park where Lake Ontario and the Niagara River meet. Old Fort Niagara on the USA side would stand as an approving sentinel behind us.

That Friday night, after finishing my chores, I picked up Gerda in Burlington, and together we headed to her parents' home. With much purpose and excitement, I suggested we drive through the streets of Niagara-on-the-Lake toward the lake.

Nothing went as planned.

The sun had already set and it was unusually cold for July. Gerda wanted to go home. When I pulled into the parking lot by the lake, she demanded, "What are you doing?"

"I want to go for a walk with you and see the lights at the Fort."

"It's way too chilly," she objected, irritated, and grimaced at the unusually dismal, cool, windy summer weather. "Besides, I'm tired. I just want to curl up and go to sleep in my bed."

Everything seemed against me, but I persisted. She resisted as I begged, "Oh, please! Let's just go for a quick walk and then straight home."

Gerda sighed. Reluctantly, she gripped her shawl tight around her shoulders and stepped out into the cold, the wind gusting around her. We pushed forward, up the embankment toward a spot in full view of the lake and the shimmering lights of Fort Niagara. I stopped and turned toward her, took hold of her hands and looked into her eyes. I was sure she could see the devotion and love in mine.

Through hair blowing around her face, she squinted at me with a quizzical look.

"Gerda, will you marry me? I have the money for a ring!" I waited for an answer with a huge smile, fully expecting to hear an affirmation.

"Oh Ian! Ian!" she said with a sigh in a pained, patient tone. "Someday I'll probably marry you, but before I say yes, I want to be absolutely sure that God is in our relationship. During hard times I don't want to be wondering if I've made a mistake. Please be patient with me."

Deflated again! Seeing her resolve, I knew there was no point in discussing the subject further. I quickly got her out of the cold and drove back to her parents' house.

That night, I lay in bed non-engaged, disappointed, and thinking, *What on earth are you waiting for? It's so obvious we are meant for each other! After all, this is ME you are marrying. I'll treat you like a princess, and life will be wonderful with no challenges we won't be able to overcome.*

The next morning, I was suddenly woken by a brisk knock on my bedroom door. I could tell it was morning by the glow of the light seeping in under the edges of the draperies. The door swung open. There stood Gerda, fully dressed and with a beaming smile. She swept past me to the window and threw open the curtains.

A flood of sunlight poured in as she turned and announced, "I will be happy to marry you and be your wife."

Flabbergasted at her sudden change of heart, I sputtered, "What . . . what happened?" At the same time, I was so pleased I couldn't stop grinning. Gerda, still smiling mysteriously, evidently enjoyed watching my cascading emotions. She sat down on the bed and motioned for me to sit up.

"I woke up early this morning and prayed about what to say because I went to sleep believing now was completely the wrong time to get engaged," she said.

"Then I remembered the four decision-making points in Paul Little's booklet, *Affirming the Will of God.* He says when circumstances, the counsel of others, God's Word, and our desire all line up, then we know that the thing we are considering is God's will."

I listened in amazement.

"I knew the first two were in place, since you had money for a ring and all our family and friends were supporting our relationship. But I didn't have confirmation from God's

Word, and I didn't really want to be engaged. So, two out of four meant no at that point.

"Then the birds began to sing, and I fell asleep again. I had peace about what I said to you last night. A little while later, I woke up and picked up my Bible. When I got to 2 Corinthians 8:24, the words leaped off the page at me: '*Wherefore, show yourself to them and before the churches, the proof of your love...*' "

"Ian," she said, her eyes dancing with joy, "I believe God was talking to me about our relationship! I had just read another chapter in the same book where it said, "...confirm your love toward him." Her face was glowing with excitement.

God had given Gerda the confirmation she needed, and suddenly she *wanted* to be engaged. She couldn't wait to tell me.

I was overwhelmed with thoughts and emotions with this new development, especially considering our track record.

As soon as I recovered enough to take action, we made plans to go to St. Catharines and look for an engagement ring. Gerda had prayed she would know the right ring when she saw it. We went into a few shops and returned to buy one from the second store we had visited. A fifteen percent discount that day brought it to nine dollars less than I had budgeted. Pretty much all I had!

The ring had one of the smallest diamonds ever, set with two small side stones on a gold band. It was simple, elegant, and fitted with temporary sizing beads so we could walk out of Howarth's Jewellery with Gerda proudly wearing it for the world to see.

She was thrilled, and her joy made me happy. She always loved that ring, even in later years when I bought her a much more valuable one.

It didn't take long for the world to notice. When we left the store, we unexpectedly met Gerda's parents. We had left that morning without sharing our plans, or knowing theirs.

Gerda's mother asked casually, "So what are you two up to?"

Gerda, ready to explode with the news, immediately held up her hand to them: "We're engaged!"

They were very excited to hear our news, gave Gerda a big hug, and congratulated us both.

"Why don't we see if we can find you a new dress to celebrate?" Gerda's dad suggested. She didn't need to be asked twice. We walked down the street to Susan Miles dress shop, and Gerda found her perfect dress quickly. Her dad gifted her with it.

Since it was Gerda's birthday weekend as well, we went gift hunting. She wrote in her diary, "Without really looking, we came across a beautiful brass lamp-candle, not electric, at twenty percent off."

What a spectacular birthday weekend! An engagement, a ring, a dress, and a gift!

Gerda wrote, "God just walked before us." I couldn't have agreed more. Years later, I learned she was very careful with purchases and rarely bought things hastily. It had been a record shopping day.

Back at home, Annie, Gerda's best friend, called to wish Gerda a happy birthday. After they had chatted for a while, Annie said, "I know this is silly, but last night I had a dream you and Ian got engaged."

Annie knew Gerda was definitely not ready for this step and had dismissed the dream as irrelevant.

Gerda covered the mouthpiece and whispered to me, "She knows we're engaged!"

"No! That can't be!" I exclaimed. "How's that possible? We only told your parents."

Gerda, bursting with excitement, held back a little longer and let Annie keep talking.

At the right moment, she interjected softly, "Your dream is true."

I heard Annie scream. She had watched our relationship develop from my first visit in 1976 and was delighted.

It made my jaw drop to find out Annie had dreamed we were engaged. This revelation highlighted the unique and close relationship they had. They often thought alike and did similar things without knowing the other's thoughts, or intentions, like buying the same gift for each other at Christmas. They were true soul mates and maids of honour at each other's weddings.

The next day, with Gerda wearing a yellow corsage on her new summer dress, we attended her family's church service.

During the service, the pastor announced our engagement. A murmur of delight ran through the congregation and people turned to smile at us. After the meeting, we were inundated with well-wishers expressing their love and support.

That afternoon, to celebrate Gerda's birthday and our engagement, we went for a picnic in Queenston Heights Park with Annie and her husband Gerry. Echoing Gerda's heart's desire to know God intimately, Annie had framed a pressed pansy arrangement as a gift and written on the back, "Psalm 3:10: *'That I may know Him.'* "

We immediately started making preliminary wedding plans. With most of my family and friends living in the United Kingdom, we decided on a twelve-month engagement to allow reasonable time for them to make travel arrangements.

So, five years after Gerda and I first met in Montreal, our wedding date was set for July 25, 1981.

Johannes, my friend whom I met years ago in Montreal, wherever you are in the world, thank you! You helped set the course of my forty-three-year adventure with Gerda, my forever sweetheart and wife!

CHAPTER 8

The Wedding

On the beautiful, hot, sunny day of July 25, 1981, Gerda and I joyfully committed ourselves to each other in marriage at the United Mennonite Church in St. Catharines. Among our 220 guests were thirty-four of my family and friends from the United Kingdom.

Gerda looked gorgeous in her white chiffon gown. Dark curls under a lace-trimmed veil framed her beaming smile and sparkling green eyes. We entered the church together, her one hand tucked into the crook of my elbow, and the other holding a bouquet of red roses and lily of the valley. She was a portrait of poise and grace. Throughout the day she carried a radiant glow that brought me such joy and wonder.

Following the service, in the elegantly decorated church hall, we feasted on a delicious meal prepared by the ladies' committee. The talent of these self-taught female chefs was legendary. We devoured heaping platters of succulent roast beef, mashed potatoes with secret ingredients, farm fresh mixed veggies and coleslaw, delectable fruit squares, and ice cream.

After we laughed through speeches and clapped for musical performers taking their bows, everyone migrated to Gerda's parents' farm for an afternoon garden reception.

Between photo shoots with family and friends we mingled and enjoyed a wonderful time with our loved ones. Late in the afternoon Gerda's mother, friends and family provided a delightful buffet of traditional Mennonite appetisers and desserts including *zwieback* rolls, *koteletten*, meat cold cuts, *piroshki*, and many scrumptious treats like cheesecake, tortes, and black forest cakes.

While the festivities continued into the evening, Gerda and I slipped away with our photographer to Port Dalhousie on the shore of Lake Ontario. We had arranged for photographs to be taken with the setting sun behind us as an expression of our desire for a life filled with romantic love.

Upon our return to the celebration we changed into going-away clothes before parting from our guests and embarking on our honeymoon across the border. We planned to tour New York, Vermont, and Massachusetts. Gerda had always dreamed of visiting the New England coast, so we made our destination the picturesque seaside town of Rockport, a storybook fishing village on Cape Ann, just north of Boston.

The main attraction of this town is Bearskin Neck, a one-lane street on a point leading to a breakwall. It is lined with small, quaint nineteenth century New England cottages, each with its own tiny storefront. The street hugs the world's most "painted" harbour with its famous, red Motif #1 Lobster Shack surrounded by lobster crates and covered with buoys and fishing nets. Bays with granite rock outcroppings and sandy beaches form a rugged coastline in both directions with Front Beach, a sandy cove, right in the centre of town.

We had reservations at the Seaward Inn on Marmion Way, a quaint, beach-themed resort with exceptional hospitality and food. Mr. and Mrs. Cameron were the ultimate innkeepers. Mr. Cameron, a kind and solicitous host, attended to all our needs while Mrs. Cameron worked industriously in the background ensuring only the finest New England fare graced our table. One day when we had gone whale watching and feared we might miss dinner, we returned late to a delectable feast held for us. The food always seemed decadent with such gourmet delights as fresh-caught lobster, or creamy clam chowder. These dishes immediately became a tradition for us on future visits.

As two young people not familiar with a pampered lifestyle, nor with the services of attentive wait staff, we felt like royalty. Breakfast tempted us with its extravagance. The tantalising aroma of freshly brewed coffee lured us into the dining room, where my first course was a warm, hearty bowl of oatmeal, drenched in cream, making each bite both comforting and deeply satisfying. Next came the main course: bacon and eggs prepared in various ways, accompanied by a variety of delicious sides. Finally, oven-fresh muffins, topped with whipped cream, rounded off this indulgent meal. I loved every bite of it! By the end of breakfast, I was in heavenly bliss.

Our accommodations also were "divine." We were given the room "Breakers Three," in a charming, two-storey, clapboard New England house across the street from the main inn. With only four bedrooms, it was a perfect retreat. From our second-floor room we were awed by an unobstructed and breathtaking ocean view. The house stood only fifty yards from the rugged rock edge overlooking the Atlantic. Our days there were glorious.

I remember so clearly the beautiful, sunny days with Gerda lounging on the bed engrossed in a book as the sheer curtains billowed gently in the warm sea breeze. For her that was a "sublime" experience—precious time filled with happy memories.

The day before we were scheduled to leave, we asked the assistant manager, Bob, if there was a possibility of staying another night. We didn't have any expectations. Every day, we saw people walking in asking for accommodations and receiving the same response: "Sorry, we're full." That's exactly the reply we received.

The following morning, with our car packed, we sat in the dining room, basking in the tantalising aromas and bites of our last breakfast and reminiscing wistfully on our stay at the Seaward Inn. Mr. Cameron came to our table. We expected him to say goodbye, but instead he leaned in close and said softly, "I heard you were hoping to stay another day. The inn is full, but we could offer you something. It's a room my wife and I use in the winter. As long as you don't mind some of our personal items being there. Would that be okay?"

Gerda and I glanced at each other in disbelief. She broke out in a great smile. I could feel her enthusiasm.

"Absolutely, yes!" I declared. "What a kind offer! We're so happy and grateful!"

In the end, we came back to him three days in a row asking to stay "just one more night." Finally, when our limited budget was completely depleted, we reluctantly said farewell to this very special place filled with so many wonderful memories.

Over the years, we returned to Rockport many times for our tenth, fifteenth, and twentieth anniversaries, as well as on other occasions. It was our favourite place on Earth, until our trip to Israel. That country, with its rich history, fascinating archaeological sites, and deep spiritual roots, stole Gerda's heart. However, Rockport continues to be my most beloved place, holding a special place in my heart.

CHAPTER 9

Family

Family came much sooner than planned. Five weeks before Gerda gave birth, an ultrasound revealed that she was carrying twins. Twins didn't run in either family. It was a big surprise.

The next jolt came when they arrived two months early. Thus, only one year and four days after our wedding we were blessed with beautiful, identical twin girls: Susan weighed three pounds, twelve ounces and Elizabeth (Liz) three pounds, six ounces. Such joy and disruption suddenly dropped on us! That day is so clear in my memory.

Gerda had finished teaching for the summer, and I came home to join her for lunch. I proudly showed her a new alphanumeric display pager I had picked up that morning. Before we ate, I gave her a full explanation and demonstration. I told her it would always be on me, and if she went into labour, she could just call the paging service. I would instantly be notified and come running. A few minutes later, as we started eating, Gerda's water broke. She was in labour!

We threw some overnight necessities into a small suitcase and raced to Joseph Brant Hospital in Burlington. Dr. Barry Hunter quickly assessed her condition and determined that the best care for her and the babies would be provided at McMaster University Hospital in Hamilton, which was better equipped to handle the complexities of premature, multiple births. We were transferred by ambulance, and Gerda was assigned under the care of Dr. Molly Towel and her team of at least ten doctors, doctors-in-training, and nurses for these high-risk deliveries. Thankfully, I was allowed to stay with her.

The births were challenging, as expected, but not just because the babies were premature. They were also breech—arriving bottom first, rather than head first. In addition, once they were born it was discovered that in the womb they experienced twin-to-twin transfusion syndrome (TTTS), meaning blood had drained from one baby into the other. Baby Elizabeth (Liz) was born a rosy red due to too much blood, and Susan, snow white with insufficient blood. We later learned that their premature births probably saved their lives, since only ten to fifteen percent of babies with TTTS survive if they aren't treated in time.

Our miracle babies faced several challenges. They were immediately whisked away for blood transfusions. Without fully developed lungs, they required oxygen and were also placed under phototherapy lights to treat jaundice. Due to their frailty, they received medical and nutritional treatments intravenously. IV needles were often sticking out of various parts of their tiny bodies, and we were not permitted to hold them. We looked helplessly into their incubators, unable to do anything but pray.

The medical help was exceptional. We were so grateful we could receive care at the NICU (Neonatal Intensive Care Unit) of this world-renowned hospital. Once the babies stabilised, they were transferred back to Joseph Brant in Burlington.

While the girls were in hospital, my life revolved around daily visits. Gerda barely left their side, sleeping at the hospital to watch over them and learn as much as possible about care for these tiny, delicate humans.

Six weeks after our dear daughters arrived in the world, we welcomed them home, and the survival games began. Ours, that is! The babies were fine.

When the girls came home, life took on the nature of a rollercoaster travelling at breakneck speed, jarring us around sharp corners and down scary, steep slopes we didn't see coming. Everything was a blur, especially at night when Gerda kept one baby in the main bedroom to breastfeed, while I took care of the other in the second bedroom. We exchanged babies on alternate nights so they would both get the benefit of their mother's milk, and the skilful, undivided attention of their father-in-training.

To say each night was an adventure would be an understatement. The girls were flyweights and had a lot of growing to do to catch up with full-term babies. They awakened up to eight times a night to be fed, diapered, and have their sleepers changed. By morning my "baby-of-the-night" had consumed three to four eight-ounce bottles of formula and had accumulated a pile of dirty diapers and sleepers on the floor.

Gerda's nightly ordeal yielded similar results, so each morning a small mountain of clothes was ready for washing. That's when we really appreciated the diaper service Gerda's brother John and his future wife, Susan, had gifted us. Like a small miracle, dirty diapers disappeared out the door and returned nice and clean a few days later.

With much love, support, and help from family and friends, especially my mother-in-law, we survived. Each week Gerda's mother drove to Burlington from St. Catharines and brought many delicious dishes to sustain us. She stayed three or four days to do household chores and help care for the babies. Oma sat in the rocking chair, snuggled them in her arms, sang to them, and rocked them back and forth. It's not surprising the girls developed a strong bond with her and retained that special relationship throughout her life.

Friends Patti McLennan and Brenda Ralph also came by each week to help with never-ending chores. Many helped us make it through those challenging days while I worked at my fledgling real estate business launched four months prior to their birth. I must admit, work provided me with a much-needed break, and on more than one occasion I rested my head on my desk to sleep. Such peace! Stolen quiet moments! Pure bliss!

Three-and-a-half years after the girls were born we were thrilled to welcome David into our family. What a huge contrast his birth was to the first one! He weighed in at a healthy seven pounds, twelve ounces, a birth weight more than that of his sisters combined. Under the guidance of Dr. Andrew Magee-Davey, David's entry into the world was much less dramatic, with only two health-care practitioners present, compared to ten or more with the girls.

I shared this observation with Gerda while she was still in the hospital, and she agreed that David's birth had been far less stressful than Susan and Liz's. She made it crystal clear, however, that if I wanted any more children, I was welcome to give birth to them myself.

I don't recall ever discussing that topic again.

CHAPTER 10

Storm Clouds

Life was good! Really good! Or, at least I thought so. Sadly, I was oblivious to storm clouds gathering in my relationship with my wife, whom I loved passionately. Looking back, I now see that cracks were already forming early in our marriage.

During the summer of 1986, five years into our marriage, I clearly remember Gerda getting very upset with me over some unkind and uncaring comments I unwittingly made. At the time, I didn't fully understand or appreciate the challenges she faced in balancing the demands of family life alongside the unrealistic expectations I placed on her. It didn't occur to me that I may need to change something about myself. Sadly, any heartfelt communication she tried to express to me fell on deaf ears. Eventually, I came to understand why my comments were so upsetting to her, and how I wish I could go back and relive that time with the wisdom I have today.

In 1980, when I had arrived in Canada, I worked on the dairy farm. Part of my responsibility was to care for and milk the Canadian Holstein cows. At that time, Gerda and I were not yet married. We were planning our future together and soon realised we had a major conundrum.

Regardless of how Gerda tried to endure the farm stench that clung to me, she just couldn't tolerate it. Before we spent any time together I would shower thoroughly, scrub my hands, and douse myself with deodorant, but I just couldn't pass her smell test. She would often burst into tears because of the "unbearable" farm odour emanating from me. Many times she couldn't even hold my hand. Quickly it became apparent that if I wanted to marry the woman of my dreams, milking cows couldn't be in my future. Consequently, two weeks before our wedding, I left farm life behind once and for all. Trusting this would allow sufficient time for any agrarian aroma to dissipate from my body before our special day.

At the time of our wedding I didn't have a new job, but I had an idea of what I could do. Before I had moved to Canada, for almost three years, I had worked in real estate as an estate agent for Humberts in Southampton. Gerda and I had considered real estate work as a possibility for me, but it had some drawbacks. The main one was remuneration, and the other, the hours one is expected to work. In England I was paid a salary and worked from 9:00 a.m. until 5:00 p.m. Monday to Friday, and every second Saturday until 1:00 p.m. In Canada, pay was one hundred percent commission, with an on-call schedule for any time of day or night, seven days a week. These working terms made us think a job as a real estate agent wouldn't work for us as newlyweds who wanted to focus on building a strong marriage.

Five months after our wedding I was still without work, so we decided to revisit the real estate option. As a result, on April 1, 1982, after completing the necessary courses, I started my real estate career at the Burlington office of an independent brokerage called Bayley MacLean. Clare MacLean, one of the founding partners, worked at the Oakville office and became a cherished mentor and friend. He took me under his wing and blessed me with sage advice as well as lots of encouragement. When he passed away in 2008, the *Oakville Beaver* described Clare as "The Elder Statesman in the Oakville Real Estate Community." He was greatly loved and respected by so many—the ultimate real estate professional—and above all, he was a man of faith, great integrity, and somebody I wanted to emulate.

In my new career as a real estate agent, I faced several challenges, and I appreciated Clare's mentoring. At the time, Canada was experiencing a major economic recession with interest rates exceeding twenty percent. As a result, many homes were for sale, but there were very few buyers. Being new in the country, I lacked a social network from which to draw potential clients. My relationships were limited to Gerda and a few of her friends in the Burlington area. Despite these challenges, I came home on the last day of my first month with a sale. I am forever grateful to Al and Heather Germain for entrusting me with their purchase and my first transaction!

Those early years were lean. We had to count every penny twice before spending it. We continued to be blessed with sales, and every bill was paid, even with Gerda resigning from her teaching position following her maternity leave with the twins. The number of sales surprised us. Soon I was recognised as one of the highest producing individual real estate agents in my office and then in my company across Canada. Later, after I built my own real estate team, we achieved similar industry recognition.

With a need to provide for my family, and an awareness that past performance does not guarantee future results, I worked diligently. Real estate was my "sweet spot," and I never found it hard to go to work. To this day I love helping people fulfil their home ownership dreams.

Because of my farming and tourism industry background, I was accustomed to working long hours. Without realising it, I spent more and more time away from home—a perfect recipe for marital discord. As a result, my family suffered from neglect. It was the very last thing I wanted to inflict upon them, but sadly, I did.

My relationship with my beautiful bride was suffering, and I didn't know it. My blinders were firmly in place covering the "eyes of my understanding." I couldn't see that Gerda was feeling abandoned and alone while I threw myself into serving my clients and our church community. Eventually I started to realize that our marital difficulties were not rooted in my workaholic tendencies alone, but also in my inability to accept the differences in our personalities. As with many relationships, opposites attract, and we were a classic case.

Gerda was a deep thinker, and I was all about action.

She liked to read, and I liked to explore.

She was an introvert (energised by solitude), and I was an extrovert (energised by interaction with people).

Her "love languages" were time and conversation, and mine was touch.

She loved quiet walks, and I loved climbing mountains.

The list of opposites went on and on.

Initially we were attracted because our differences complemented one another, but later they became irritating. Instead of drawing us together, they pushed us apart, especially because I lacked an awareness of the effect of my actions. Without realising it, I wanted her to become more like me.

One day, in my zeal, I purchased bicycles for all of us so we could become a "cycling family." It seemed like a great idea, but cycling wasn't Gerda's thing, and I was essentially trying to change her into what I wanted her to be. I see now I was disrespecting her by not accepting her for who she was and especially by not involving her in any discussion before going ahead with my plans.

Another situation arose with roots that went as far back as our honeymoon in Rockport.

Every day I had been excited to explore something new about that beautiful, small, fishing village with its many treasures. I often explored it alone on an early morning run or midday hike. One day, after I had returned to our room following one of these outings, I found Gerda immersed in a book. With great enthusiasm, I shared my discoveries and invited her to join me immediately on another excursion.

"That sounds interesting," she smiled. "Let's do it later. Right now I really want to stay and finish my book."

I couldn't understand, or accept, that she didn't want to go with me *immediately* to see this amazing new discovery of mine. I was frustrated, shocked, disappointed, and walked away sulking because I had to wait. I realise now I had acted with nothing more than good old-fashioned self-centredness and immaturity.

I went away and cooled my jets. Later, Gerda was more than happy to share the excitement of discovery with me.

As I look back, it's easy to see that my reaction was like that of an emotional adolescent and resulted from my lack of understanding and acceptance of our personality differences. As time went on, my inability to cherish her for who she was, combined with my workaholic tendencies, set our marital ship on course for shipwreck.

CHAPTER 11

Rebuilding

Years later Gerda confided that during those early years of marriage she came to realise that her destiny was to live an emotionally lonely life from me. With me busy helping others and demonstrating a critical spirit toward her, she felt isolated, unaccepted, and unloved. It was a truly tragic commentary on our relationship, even though I was trying to love her with all my heart.

Before we met I had been preparing for marriage by closely observing friends with wonderful marriages, people like Mike and Chris Treneer, Issam and Abla Khoury and Martin and Marion Cooper. I read books on how to have a great marriage, because I deeply desired a fairy tale where we would "live happily ever after." But that wasn't happening. My fragile ego was blocking me from accepting my sweetheart's words of correction and from listening to her appeal for a better understanding of her needs. Despite our inner turmoil, I bulldozed on, blind to any threat to our relationship.

Around the six-year mark we started to seek help. In my view, it wasn't for our marriage. I didn't see there was much wrong with it. Rather, I saw it as for my dear wife, who was struggling with some troubling thoughts and fears.

In our quest for help we met with the senior pastor of our church, Ron Gannet. He shared some helpful insights about how past experiences often influence us with negative thoughts and actions even when we want nothing to do with them.

In the corner of his office where we sat, there was a small tree with a gnarly and twisted trunk. Ron pointed to the tree trunk and explained that traumas in life sometimes negatively affect us and result in crooked (unhealthy) thinking and behaviour patterns. We were affected just like the tree trunk that had not grown straight and strong. He encouraged us, that with patience and guidance, these struggles could be overcome and referred us to a counsellor: Jessie Cooper.

Jessie, like one of God's angels, became a guardian of our relationship. She was Gerda's trusted confidante, and interestingly, mine too. I drove with Gerda to the early sessions, and during our trip home she would debrief me on their time together. On the first two drives, Gerda was very frustrated.

"Jessie just doesn't get it," she insisted, convinced Jessie did not understand her situation and struggles. Fortunately, she persevered, and little by little began to realise Jessie did understand after all.

After three or four months, Gerda began to gain freedom from the lies she had believed. As truth replaced them, she became less anxious and fearful.

Around that time, Jessie invited me into one of the sessions, and after that I started receiving my own counselling with her. With gentle and skilful questions she probed my past for emotionally painful experiences. To my utter surprise, I discovered deep emotional pain, especially from a childhood incident. Jessie prayerfully spoke the love of Jesus into that hurtful memory and brought inner healing into parts of my soul I didn't know had been affected.

As I continued in counselling, Jessie helped enlighten my mind considerably. I was shocked to understand that I had a big part to play in Gerda's pain and was the reason for many of her issues. Primarily, my heart was not fully committed to her and our home, and I was not fully accepting of her for who she was. When I started realising these truths, I set out to win back the heart of my sweetheart by acknowledging my failures, asking for forgiveness, and seeking to change my behaviour.

I learned that changing beliefs and habits takes time. For me, it was slow progress with many setbacks, especially because of my insecurities that resisted correction. A situation comes to mind concerning Thursday mornings.

Each Thursday morning I attended a men's Bible study and prayer group and refused to miss it even if Gerda needed help at home with the children. One day, however, I skipped the meeting to go skiing with my brother Duncan, who was visiting from overseas. Not surprisingly, Gerda was upset. She saw I would miss a meeting for someone else, but not for her. When she told me how it made her feel, I couldn't validate her feelings. Instead I justified my actions, saying it wasn't often that I saw my brother.

Understanding slowly dawned on me. I realised she was right to feel the way she did, so I stopped attending the Thursday morning meetings to help her with the children instead. Four months later I was surprised when Gerda encouraged me to re-join the group. When I was convinced she was totally comfortable with that decision, I started re-attending, but never again hesitated missing a meeting if she needed me.

I continued working at loving Gerda the way she needed to be loved. One morning, more than twelve months after I had started counselling sessions, we were in bed when she said softly, "I think you are starting to change."

I was shocked and angry, but thankfully I held my tongue. Saying anything in the moment would have undoubtedly undermined the progress we'd been making.

She slipped out of bed, put on her housecoat, and went downstairs to start her day. As soon as she left, I turned on my side, livid, punched the pillow next to me to vent my anger, and screamed in my head; *You only THINK I am beginning to change? After all I have done for you in the past year?* I was exasperated. She was only *just starting* to accept that I loved her unconditionally.

Since that time, I have come to understand how easy it is to make emotional withdrawals from someone's life through hurtful words and actions, and how hard it is to repair the damage they cause and rebuild broken trust.

Despite my emotional setback, I was determined to continue loving her without reservation. Gerda showed immeasurable grace toward me, especially once she was convinced my heart was committed to her and our home. She later shared her response to an incident that helped solidify this new-found trust.

It occurred the day I came home with a pull-out cabinet organiser for a small cupboard space by the kitchen sink. Not only did I bring it home, but I also installed it—a major feat considering I'm not a handyman.

She had mentioned the small, non functional section of kitchen cabinets before, and it meant a lot to her that I took the initiative to address it without her needing to ask. My action showed that I had truly listened to her needs and responded thoughtfully, which was a new experience for her.

Rebuilding love for one another was slow, but we worked at it every way possible through marriage courses and taking time away together. By God's grace, we built a marriage that became more beautiful and precious than we could have imagined. Most importantly, we always sought to align our lives with the things that truly mattered by prioritising everything we did in the order of God, family, then business.

CHAPTER 12

God, Family, Then Business

"God, Family, *Then* Business" is the values statement of Keller Williams, the world's largest real estate franchise company. I took a position there at age fifty-nine, and for the very first time in more than thirty-seven years in the workforce, I was working for a company that prioritises the importance of spirituality. They believe it is the best foundation for success in every aspect of life, including business. Gary Keller and Jay Papasan expand on this truth in their book, T*he One Thing*. It has sold three million copies and translated into forty languages.

While I was growing up, spirituality was a mystery to me. I had been told humans are three-part beings of body, mind, and spirit. Body and mind I could understand, but not spirit. I had no understanding of it at all, despite having been baptised as a baby, confirmed when I was twelve, and having attended church almost every Sunday until I was fifteen.

However I had three intriguing experiences indicating there was more to life than just the body and mind.

When I was seven or eight years old, my mother became gravely ill, and I was terrified she was going to die. I cried out to God, praying for her survival, but once the crisis was passed, I moved on with life. It is the only time I recall praying, until many years later.

On another occasion, as a fourteen-year-old, I was climbing Mount Helvellyn in England's Lake District with a teacher and a small group of students from my school. About three-quarters of the way up the mountain, we stopped for a break. For some reason I slipped away by myself and found a ridge with a stunning view down the mountain to Glenridding, which looked like a child's miniature village in the distance.

It was a warm, beautiful sunny day. The view was breathtaking, with a handful of clouds dancing across the sky—a perfect Lake District day with visibility for miles, especially from my vantage point. I was mesmerised by the beauty of the lush green grasslands surrounding Glenridding, the glistening Ullswater Lake in the background, and the rugged, austere mountains framing it.

The serenity of this tranquil scene settled on me and wrapped me in a profound, otherworldly peace. Suddenly, a question started reverberating through my mind and continued to echo: *What is it all about? What is it all about? What is it all about?* It was as if the mountains themselves were calling out to me. The peculiar incident didn't frighten me, but I sensed I had been drawn into an unusual out-of-body experience. I quickly shook off the trance-like state and hurried to re-join my friends.

The third event occurred four years later when one of my best friends drowned while swimming in the River Lune, near Lancaster. After my buddies and I attended Robin's funeral, we went on a pub crawl to numb the pain of our grief. As we transitioned from one pub to another, we jokingly commented that we believed Robin was looking down on us as we partied.

I clearly remember the impact of these three incidents and now believe that something more significant may have been happening than I realised at the time.

- In fear of losing someone special, I was reaching out for supernatural intervention through prayer.
- Through the wonder of creation, I was questioning the purpose of life.
- In the midst of grief, I was seeking eternity.

In each case, once these moments passed, I gave very little to no further consideration to them. None led me on a quest for answers to the purpose of life, or in search of anything spiritual, but now I realise they were preparing me for my journey ahead.

In 1973, a year after I lost my friend Robin, I left my hometown of Morecambe to attend Southampton College of Technology for a three-year Estate Management course studying real estate law and valuations, property management, town planning and general construction. During Freshman Week at the local university, I met Howard Sheffield, an engineer who spent his spare time working with a student ministry called the Navigators. That day, he was asking students survey-style questions about their understanding of faith and spirituality. He explained what he was doing, and I warily agreed to participate.

The questionnaire was brief, and I was puzzled by what seemed like weird questions concerning my thoughts on spiritual matters. I didn't have much to say.

I so clearly remember one question: "If you were to die today and stand before God, and God said to you, 'What have you done to merit coming into Heaven?' what would you say?"

I thought for a moment and replied, "Well, if God exists and there really is a Heaven, then I guess it's up to him who gets in. I'd have nothing to say about it."

This answer, and others, indicated I had zero belief in God and little interest in the topic.

I was very thankful for the way my parents had raised me. By their good example and training in morals and values, I was a caring, considerate person who respected authority and others. In my mind, what else did I need? Life was very good. At nineteen years of age, and 275 miles from my parents' reach, I was profoundly enjoying the freedom college life offered. I envisioned an exciting path ahead with many new relationships and opportunities waiting to be explored. Seeking God definitely wasn't one of them. I had absolutely no idea it could be a potential adventure.

At the end of the questionnaire, Howard asked me if I would like to attend a small group study to see how Jesus could interface with my daily life. I shrugged my shoulders and said, "I don't know."

"That's okay," he said. "If you are not interested, neither are we." His response took me aback, and I surprised myself by saying, "Okay I'll do it."

For the next few months, I engaged in some investigative Bible studies and heard what to me seemed like far-fetched ideas. The craziest one was that Jesus claimed to be God and said he would die and be raised from the dead after three days. I agreed with C.S. Lewis's observation in his book, *Mere Christianity* that Jesus could not be just a moral teacher. He either had to be a liar, a lunatic—similar to someone who thinks he's a poached egg—or he was exactly who he claimed to be. In my opinion, the crucial question was whether he had risen from the dead or not. If he had, it would prove he was a man of his word, which meant I would have to give serious consideration not just to this claim, but also everything else he said.

When I investigated the facts surrounding the resurrection, I concluded that I would need more faith to believe Jesus had *not* risen than to believe he had. As a result, soon after my twentieth birthday, I prayed my first heartfelt prayer since I was a young boy. In this simple and short prayer, I acknowledged that I believed in Jesus and cautiously committed myself to being his follower. It wasn't a profound prayer or experience, but it was the start of my journey toward an intimate relationship with God.

At fourteen, Gerda made a similar life-changing decision, giving her a greater understanding of life's purpose and meaning. Throughout high school and the rest of her life, she sought to personalise the question that was also the title of one of her favourite books, *How Should We Then Live*, by Frances Schaeffer. In whatever role she found herself, whether as a student, daughter, sibling, teacher, wife, mother, family member, friend or neighbour, she passionately pursued the answer to this question. She never wavered from seeking to know God's heart in good times or bad.

Gerda as a five-year-old; always a class act!

Me as a four year old, looking for my next adventure..

One of my favourite photos of Gerda.

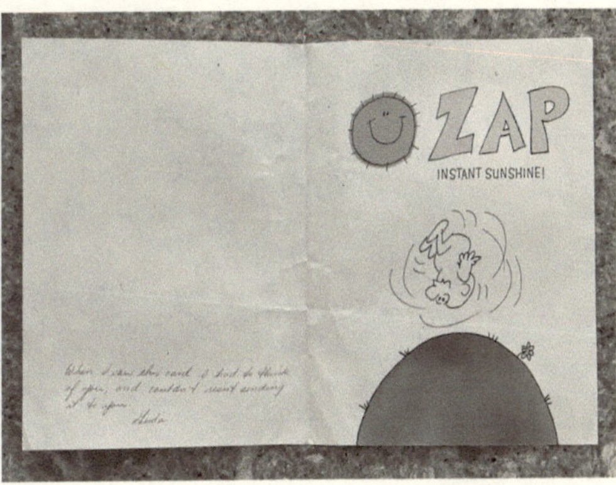

The card Gerda sent back to me in 1976 declining my request to be her boyfriend.

The photo I shared with my friends and family in 1979 to introduce them to Gerda.

Gerda wearing the dress her dad bought her in celebration of our engagement in 1980.

The day I'd dreamed of for many years.

Our first photo on Lake Ontario.

Heading off on our honeymoon adventure!

The highlight of our honeymoon, Seaward Inn, Rockport.

Gerda, an insatiable reader... even on our honeymoon!

Enjoying a leisurely breakfast in the early days of our marriage.

Gerda glowing as a mother, radiant with love for her family.

Basking in the buttercup fields of England.

Family adventure at Webster Falls, Dundas.

Revisiting our very special room inside "The Breakers".

Gerda enjoying the Atlantic ocean outside our treasured accommodation.

Family holiday in the sun.

Gerda always felt a sense of freedom at the oceans edge.

Beach time together.

PART II

CHAPTER 13

The Best Christmas Ever

In the fall of 2018, Gerda was unable to lift her arm above her head. Initially her doctor thought it might be a pinched nerve, but when Gerda was still experiencing discomfort several months later, she booked her for a CT scan. In the aftermath, the doctor's office requested an in-person appointment to discuss the results. We were apprehensive.

For five years Gerda had been taking tests regularly due to a bout with breast cancer in 2013. At that time, she had had a small tumour removed from her left breast. Nine months after undergoing chemotherapy, she was declared cancer free. This was the first time she had been called to the doctor's office to hear results, so I made myself available to accompany her. Dr. Janice Witcher greeted us, and when we were seated, immediately addressed the purpose of the visit.

"I am sorry to say I have some unfortunate news. The cancer has returned. It's now in your bones, lungs, and liver, and there is a mass around your left shoulder."

The news was devastating. I glanced at Gerda. She was looking at the doctor calmly, listening and not betraying any emotions.

"How long do I have?" she asked matter-of-factly.

"It could be six to nine months…" she hesitated a little, "...maybe as much as a year or two, depending on how you respond to treatments."

I suspect she added the last statement to give us hope because of the tears that were already pouring down my face in a manner I didn't know was possible. Gerda! My sweetheart! My wife whom I had come to love so deeply, had just been given a death sentence! I had never imagined such a thing could happen.

The doctor explained that she would arrange for us to meet with an oncologist to discuss treatment options. Gerda sat quietly, taking in the information.

Then she said, "If this is my time to go, I'm okay with it. I'm so thankful for so much, especially my family. It's been a wonderful life filled with so many blessings. I have no regrets. And most importantly, I know where I will spend eternity."

While Gerda seemed calm and very composed, I couldn't say a word. Tears kept flowing. I was numb with shock. The doctor's words were tumbling in my mind. My thoughts rushed this way and that to find solutions that just weren't there.

"How are you doing, Ian?" Dr. Witcher asked gently. My mind on autopilot, I gave one of my classic one-liners: "I'm okay, thank you!"

We thanked the doctor for her time as we left. We always appreciated her compassionate care, and never more so than during this dark time.

The next few days were a blur of grief as we grappled with the implications of this unthinkable situation. My thoughts were still crashing about, running into walls that had suddenly appeared. How quickly life could turn! The hardest thing to comprehend was the extent to which the disease was ravaging Gerda's body. Externally there was no evidence of it, except for the limited use of her arm.

The day prior to the appointment with Dr Witcher, on December 10, we had returned from a magical four-day trip to New York City with our daughter Susan, son-in-law Jordan, and three grandchildren, Makayla, Liam, and Julia. We had taken in so many of the wonderful sights and Christmas festivities for which this city is famous, including the amazing Rockettes Christmas Spectacular at Radio City Music Hall and Santa's Village inside Macy's department store.

In the city, we travelled "New York Style"—we walked. Did we *ever* walk! With our hotel more than a mile from Times Square, each day we trekked for miles.

We walked to Rockefeller Center with its iconic Christmas tree, seventy-two feet high that year, ablaze with LED lights and embellished with three million dazzling Swarovski crystals.

We went up the Empire State Building and strolled around the enchanting Bryant Park Winter Village complete with its outdoor ice-skating rink and open air, European-style Christmas market showcasing artisans from around the world. Laughter, music, and the aroma of mouth-watering food filled the air.

We visited the sobering 9/11 Memorial, walked in Central Park, and attended a Brooklyn Tabernacle service in downtown Brooklyn, with Jim Cymbala and the world-famous Brooklyn Tabernacle Choir. The entire time *we walked and walked* and *walked*, for a total of thirty kilometres (eighteen and a half miles), with Gerda having no problem keeping pace.

How could one reconcile her healthy, vibrant appearance with that morbid diagnosis? Any thought of it seemed like a bad dream, one from which we couldn't wake up.

News got out. Shocked, horrified, grief-stricken, loving, caring family and friends rallied around us. It wasn't so much what they did or said. Their love was in their presence. Quickly, we realised we were surrounded by a mighty army of people willing to walk this journey with us.

At the end of December Gerda wrote in her diary that those were days of "shock, confusion, numbness, and peace."

Knowing her time on Earth may be short, she was distraught at the thought of missing out on future celebrations, like our grandchildren's school graduations and weddings.

We spent hours together, sometimes wrapped in each other's arms just weeping, other times praying for healing and occasionally watching Gerda's favourite cooking shows, or Hallmark Christmas movies. Most sustaining was the knowledge that "God is love" and the conviction that through heartache and uncertainty, true to Scripture, he would give us peace that passes understanding.

Christmas, Gerda's favourite time of year, would arrive only two weeks after her diagnosis. She loved absolutely everything about that season, from trimming the tree and decorating the home, to carefully selecting gifts and lovingly wrapping them. She cherished being with family and preparing an array of tantalising seasonal foods and baked treats. Among them was my all-time favourite Christmas dessert—English trifle—made with sponge cake soaked in copious amounts of sherry, layered with peaches set in Jell-O, topped with a thick layer of custard and finally finished with a generous topping of whipped cream. Absolutely delectable! I couldn't envision a more festive way to finish Christmas dinner than with a bowl or two of that delicious dessert.

With more zest and purpose than usual, Gerda immersed herself in preparations to make Christmas as special as possible. Our children were also determined to make it memorable.

Along with their children, they all huddled together and camped overnight in our home on Christmas Eve.

Gerda beamed with joy throughout those few days of celebration. She wrote in her diary, "It was so great to have all the children and grandchildren sleepover. I had bought the grandchildren Christmas PJs (pyjamas) and Susan had bought them for the grownups. What fun! They were so cosy and warm. We had pizza, salad and lots of dessert."

On Christmas morning, something magical happened. It snowed! Every year, weeks ahead of this special day, Gerda checked the weather forecast regularly hoping and praying for a white Christmas. That year, as was often the case, no snow was predicted. When it started to snow Christmas morning, she was delighted and responded with glee and wonder, thrilled that she had been granted her heart's desire.

It snowed gently throughout the day. The first words of her journal entry that day were, "The best Christmas ever! I will never forget Christmas day—snow falling lightly…." It meant so much to her. She considered it a special gift from God.

Most of all Gerda celebrated the presence of our family and friends that day. Our numbers increased from fourteen on Christmas Eve to twenty on Christmas Day and included Gerda's ninety-two-year-old mother. Through laughter and tears we shared gifts and many stories from the past. Suddenly, more conscious of the frailty of life, we sought to encourage and love each other more than before. It was a good day.

The entire time Gerda was in her element. As was her custom, she distributed mounds of gifts to everyone and absorbed their excitement as they opened them. She especially doted on the grandchildren.

Toward the end of the celebration Gerda became the centre of attention as she opened gifts from everyone. It was an unusual highlight for that to happen, and a treat for her. She was thrilled to receive a silver bracelet and more than a dozen purposefully chosen "charms" with which to adorn it from our children, grandchildren, and myself. Most pieces came with a note explaining the reason for the giver's choice. They recalled special memories like a visit to Disney World, or New York City, or something simple like eating cupcakes, having afternoon tea, or watching American Idol on TV. Each one shouted *I love you* and *Thank you for loving me!* The bracelet became her pride and joy, and from then on, it rarely left her wrist. She proudly showed it to anyone who would listen and explained its significance to herself and to the giver.

Another gift she especially cherished was a small, palm-sized wooden cross Susan gave her. She wrote in her journal: "She could have had no idea I wanted one!" The cross was always with her. Often she slept with it in her hand, or under her pillow, as a tangible reminder of God's love for her.

From the time of Gerda's diagnosis until her passing, we spent everyday together. Gerda and I appreciated each other more than ever in those days and reminisced about amazing times and experiences. Looking back, I now see this most difficult and devastating period of our lives as being wrapped in something very precious—*time*. This gift awakened us to the greatness of so many wonderful favours of grace in our lives through a myriad of loving people, and also uniquely, through the colour yellow.

CHAPTER 14

Yellow

Five months before Gerda's diagnosis, she went for a week-long respite to Wesley Acres Retreat Centre and Campground, in Prince Edward County, to hear Sharon Garlough Brown speak. Sharon had written one of Gerda's favourite book series *Sensible Shoes*—the story of four women who embarked on a spiritual journey together to seek the heart of God. She really enjoyed this series and identified well with some of the women in the books.

Gerda was very excited at the opportunity to meet Sharon and was also in desperate need of some rest and relaxation. Emotionally, physically, spiritually, she was worn out from a very busy season of assisting me with my real estate work, leading a weekly Bible study with around one hundred women, and being involved with the everyday activities of our three children and seven grandchildren. She was also doing a seventy-five-mile round trip at least once a week to help care for her independently living, wheelchair-bound mother.

Unfortunately, during the retreat the weather was rainy and unseasonably cool, so Gerda was unable to enjoy the outdoors and the beautiful lakefront setting as much as she would have liked. Her back was also bothering her, and she couldn't sit or sleep comfortably. After only three days I welcomed back a discouraged camper who craved the comforts of home and her own bed. She was very disheartened at not having experienced the time of rejuvenation she greatly needed.

However, Gerda shared two experiences she had at Wesley Acres that initially seemed insignificant but later proved pivotal during the unforeseen journey ahead.

In an early session, Sharon candidly disclosed her difficulty in believing that God really loved her. To counter this negative thought, she decided that every time she saw the colour purple, she would remember that God loves her.

Gerda identified with the same struggle. Even though she had passionately pursued God for more than fifty years, she had also found it hard to believe that God loved her. Just before she had left for the retreat, she told her friend Moira, "I've never experienced God's love." It surprised Moira, and she promised to pray daily that God would reveal it to her.

She immediately decided to appropriate Sharon's idea. *Purple is an easy colour to find,* she reasoned. *I will pick a much harder one. I'll choose the colour yellow, so that when-ever I see it, I'll be reminded that God loves me.*

Around the time of this session, I decided to send her some flowers. I called a florist close to the campground and explained my intentions. The gentleman asked me what I would like to send. I replied "Flowers! You choose from what you have in stock". I then proceeded to tell him the amount I wanted to spend, provided my credit card details, and gave him her cabin number.

Gerda told me about the flowers with some amazement. "You know what colour they were? Yellow! Mostly yellow!"

Interestingly, a few years later I discovered a photograph of the flowers on her phone camera. I could see a few yellow flowers in the bouquet, but more significantly, they were in a vase wrapped in a large yellow bow.

We had no idea that this seemingly innocuous event was the start of something far greater than we could have ever imagined.

As the sobering reality of Gerda's diagnosis fully set in, we sought the next steps in her treatment.

CHAPTER 15

Next Steps

My dear wife knew the bitter taste of chemotherapy from her bout with cancer in 2013. Due to adverse side effects from every round of treatment, including shingles, she was leaning away from taking chemotherapy, preferring quality of life over the possibility of extra time. We continued waiting for appointments and information from our local health-care providers regarding options.

On January 16, 2019, our daughter Liz booked us an appointment with Dr. Agnes Matacz, a naturopathic doctor. She recommended Dr. Herzog's Hospital in Germany where they combine conventional medicine with a range of complementary, naturopathic treatments to support the immune system. One of the main treatments was whole-body hyperthermia combined with chemotherapy.

We learned that cancer cells don't like heat, so under general anaesthesia, the patient's body temperature is raised to a fever pitch. While the cancer cells are in a weakened state due to the fever, the patient receives a lighter than normal dose of chemotherapy. This approach resonated well with our family, so within ten days, Gerda and I were scheduled to fly to Germany.

Sadly, soon after we made this decision, Gerda's mother became ill and passed away within a few days. On January 25, we joined family and friends to honour her. It was a wonderful tribute to a life well-lived and to a loved one who expressed much love in word and deed to those around her. She was known for her caring, especially through the foods, quilts, and hand-knitted throw blankets she made for family and friends. We were reminded by her nephew Harold of the terrible heartache and hardship she endured during her upbringing. It was most fitting to sing "Amazing Grace" at her celebration of life. The words of one of the stanzas perfectly encapsulated her life, particularly while in Ukraine and on the "Great Trek." She testified about clearly witnessing God's hand of protection throughout that horrendously perilous journey as she fled her homeland:

Through many dangers, toils, and snares,
I have already come;
'Tis grace hath brought me safe thus far,
And grace will lead me home.

The day after her mother's funeral, Gerda and I set out for Germany to fight the beast of cancer, knowing that this same grace would be with us.

We flew via Iceland and arrived the next day in Bad Salzhausen, a quiet and quaint spa village for which Germany is well known. Dr. Herzog and his team immediately evaluated Gerda and started naturopathic therapy treatments to boost her immune system. They explained that a round of treatments would take about three weeks and include a wide range of natural healing processes along with the whole-body hyperthermia procedure and chemotherapy. A two-week break would follow before a repetition of this regimen.

Gerda was relieved to learn that with this program she wouldn't lose her hair, or experience the severe side effects she had in 2013. Thankfully that proved to be the case.

We spent more than three months at Dr. Herzog's hospital with a two-week break to return to Canada between the second and third treatments.

During our time in Germany, we were blessed with many heartfelt expressions of love and support from our family and friends. One of the most unique and meaningful gifts was a handmade quilt from our friend Janice Cameron. After Janice had sewn it together, she took it to family and friends for them to write messages of encouragement and blessing on it. Gerda was thrilled with it, especially as she was able to read the many heartfelt comments people had written. This quilt truly lived up to its name as a "comforter" because of the love, support, and prayers embedded in it. From the day she received it, she often snuggled under it, and it remained on her bed no matter where the bed might be.

Another special memory was of our visitors, including my youngest brother Duncan, who rearranged a UK business trip via Germany and flew in to see us from Fredericton, New Brunswick.

The greatest joy was a visit from our three children, Susan's husband Jordan, and five of our grandchildren who definitely would have earned the "guest of honour" award, had one been given.

Grandchildren always brought Gerda so much cheer and delight. Their presence was like a refreshing ocean breeze on a sunny day. We dined together in the hospital dining room, strolled through the parks, and watched them sing and dance on the open air theatre stage. We watched with joy as they squealed with delight riding the rocking donkey near one of our favourite cafés, savoured delicious *gelato*, and indulged in scrumptious tortes that Germany is renowned for.

We were so grateful spring came early. When we first arrived, the weather was cold and damp and reminded me of the climate I was used to in England. Several times we awakened to a dusting of snow that disappeared by noon. But in the middle of February, just in time for the arrival of our family, the temperatures started rising. It became unseasonably warm, well above average for that time of year, and remained so for the rest of our time there.

As the weather warmed, we started enjoying strolls around the village. In the parks we noticed trees and bushes beginning to blossom, and by the time our family arrived, we strolled around the beautiful public grounds with floral gardens ablaze in vibrant colour.

Early February arrived with a burst of yellow from a huge forsythia just outside the hospital dining room window. For more than two months, an unusually long time, it exploded with colour, and each day we gazed at its golden-yellow beauty at mealtimes.

Sunny yellow pansies lifted their heads in the flower beds along the driveway and footpath leading to the hospital entrance. In the park gardens, along with hosts of golden daffodils, their bobbing yellow faces in bright clusters met the eye everywhere we turned. We were totally surrounded by the colour yellow, an observation that didn't escape my sweetheart.

"What colour are the hospital walls," she asked mischievously one day, looking across the room at them. I had to look, but sure enough! They were yellow. Not only that, but I noticed the exterior walls were also yellow, a rarity in the village.

We talked about the overwhelming presence of yellow in every direction. Gerda embraced this reality, marvelled at the wonder, and remembered her prayer seven months earlier at Wesley Acres Retreat Centre. She visibly drew comfort and strength in seeing it as God manifesting his presence and love for her. I believe it whispered into her heart, *I love you Gerda, you are precious in my eyes, and I am with you every step of the way.*

Our joy was multiplied when we received good news regarding the battle against her cancer. After two rounds of treatments, the tumour markers, a naturally occurring substance in the blood that indicates the presence of cancer, were reduced from ninety-five to sixty-six. The goal was to get them below thirty-five, the point at which the cancer would be deemed in remission.

After round three of treatments, the tumour markers were down to fifty—very encouraging—along with a big improvement in her mobility. When we arrived in Germany, Gerda had not been able to lift her left arm above her shoulder and now she could raise it above her head. Also, her walking endurance had increased dramatically from struggling to do a short, twenty-minute walk around the village to hours of hiking into and around the neighbouring town of Nidda.

In the midst of cautious hope, an unexpected turn of events came in the middle of May when Gerda was diagnosed with a spinal fracture. Since the cost of back surgery in Germany was very high, and with us having no insurance, the neurosurgeon strongly recommended we return to Canada as soon as possible.

We came home on the next available flight. Gerda travelled business class for the first time in her life on a seat that extended into a full-length bed so she could be as comfortable as possible. I rode economy with "visitation" privileges to check in and see how she was doing. For the first time I saw how "the other half" lived, and it looked rather nice!

The trip went well, without complications. This early return led to an unexpected season of blessing.

CHAPTER 16

The Blessing

Our return home was bittersweet. Soon after we were back, Gerda had a full-body scan that revealed she had cancer in her brain. The doctors were unable to tell if it was new growth, or previously undetected, since it was her first full-body scan. Blood tests also revealed the tumour markers had increased, letting us know the cancer had ratcheted up its campaign against her.

This news, along with awareness of the back fracture, was very disappointing. Gerda summarised her thoughts in her journal: "When I heard about the brain tumour yesterday, it was like, what else is new? It has been one thing after another!" Despite this unwelcome news, we kept battling for the healing miracle we needed, and even took a course of radiation at Juravinski Hospital in Hamilton.

During this season we took advantage of the outdoors as much as possible. Gerda always got much pleasure in our garden from orchestrating the seasonal plantings and watching the trees and flowers bloom. She also took great delight in the wide variety of birds in our backyard, with their wonderful array of stunning colours and sizes. This year was different. She was unable to garden, so we purchased season's tickets to the Royal Botanical Gardens on the boundary of Burlington and Hamilton.

Known as the RBG, it spans more than 2,400 acres on the edge of Lake Ontario and includes five gardens, as well as twenty-seven kilometres of scenic trails and 231,000 plants. It's a garden, and a nature lover's paradise, bustling with birds, bees, butterflies, and other wildlife among the gazillion flowers, shrubs, trees, and plants. One day, while we were walking around the Iris Garden with its mesmerising rainbow of colours from 960 types of blooms, I noticed a surreal quietness in Gerda, as if she were floating on clouds between the rows of flowers in a heavenly peace.

On another hot summer day, as we meandered quietly through the rose garden on the way to the tearoom, we were transported into a world of magical calm by the sweet fragrance and kaleidoscope of colours from thousands of roses.

One of our favourite stops on our way home from radiation treatments was at the Rock Garden Bistro. There we enjoyed fresh, locally sourced ingredients with our meals, many picked straight from the RBG gardens. Our preferred seating was on the covered patio close to the edge of the Rock Gardens. After our meal, we walked along the top of the former quarry with its panoramic view of the garden's lower bowl. During one of these outings, Gerda made a conscious effort to walk carefully down to the bottom of the gardens, allowing us the chance to savour the rugged beauty of the landscape and diverse flora up close, together, one last time. These were very special times for Gerda, and she often spoke of how she "craved beauty," which she found in the gardens. The day after we spent part of our wedding anniversary there, she wrote in her diary: "In front of me were some irises that were clearly out of bloom, but one plant had these beautiful, variegated leaves. As I looked at the plant, I felt God's presence. I can't describe it any other way; He was just there–no words could capture it. It has happened once before, and it comforts me immensely."

Another unexpected blessing of our early return to Canada was to be back for Mother's Day, a celebration that meant a great deal to Gerda. Prior to having children, she doubted her ability to love them the way she thought a mother should. Just after her thirtieth birthday, and before the twins arrived, she had been fully focused on her education and career without showing much interest in motherhood. She had little experience interacting with babies. Having never babysat while growing up, she worried about her ability to care for her own children. How would she respond to them? Would she possess the maternal instinct needed to be a good mother? Yet immediately upon Susan's and Liz's births, all fear disappeared, and she became a loving mother who did whatever it took to care for their welfare.

Interestingly, she had similar fears prior to our first grandchild and asked me, "How will I be able to love someone else's child?" I thought it was an odd question. This imagined angst disappeared the instant her eyes met Nya's. She cradled her in her arms, and her heart melted, overflowing with love. Later Gerda confided: "I see there's always room in my heart for one more very special person." And from then on, she enthusiastically looked forward to welcoming each one of our grandchildren: Kyenne, Makayla, Liam, Kyleigh, Julia, and Bennett. I am also sure she was cheering from Heaven at Clara and Maelyn's births.

During the late spring and summer of 2019, we enjoyed many wonderful family gatherings: Mother's Day, Father's Day, five birthday parties (including her own), plus our wedding anniversary. We were so thankful for this season of gatherings and meaningful times with family, relatives, and friends. One memorable day was our 38th wedding anniversary which Gerda captured beautifully in her journal. We began the morning with a walk along Lake Ontario, imagining we were in Rockport, with the sun shimmering like diamonds on the water. Afterward, we enjoyed a delicious lunch at The Rock Gardens Restaurant, and followed with a leisurely stroll through the gardens. That evening, after Gerda had rested for two and a half hours, our family gathered at our home to enjoy dessert and celebrate with us. As the day drew to a close, we stepped outside to say goodbye and were greeted by a breathtaking light show. The front lawn, bushes, and trees were aglow with fireflies, as if Christmas lights were draped across the branches and grass. Everyone buzzed with excitement, especially the grandchildren, as these tiny yellow glimmers of light flitted about, illuminating the summer night. It was a magnificent display and the conclusion to a truly special day reminding us of the wonder of God's creation.

Many friends from our local community visited her, as well as people from further afield, including her brother David and his wife, Gwyn. My brother Neil and his wife Janet came from England, my sister Kathy from Michigan, as well as our nephew Alistair and his wife Rachel from the USA.

Each gathering held deep significance for Gerda. She cherished every heartfelt conversation, note, and warm embrace. The love and care shown her was so profound that she said, "If I ever recover and get well, I will never be the same again." It brought me such joy to see her fully engaged in each celebration , wholeheartedly embracing and savouring every moment.

Upon reflection, I see I was already starting to grieve. I was still hoping for a miracle healing, but I was grieving the loss of doing things we had done in the past, like freely walking up and down the Rock Gardens at the RBG or taking long strolls along Lake Ontario.

That summer I got up early every morning and walked alone in our neighbourhood, often in tears, repeating the words: "This is the day the Lord has made. I will rejoice and be glad in it." I listened on my iPhone to "Morning Has Broken," sung by Cat Stevens, and a variety of John Denver's songs. One day, I stumbled upon Lauren Daigle, and very quickly, her music became a mainstay of those times, ministering deeply into my grieving heart. This early morning ritual fortified me and helped me face the day joyfully.

When I returned home from these walks, I prepared breakfast for Gerda and I to enjoy on the front porch. Those were treasured moments, tucked away and out of sight from the passing world, hidden behind a privet hedge and a huge weeping cypress on the front lawn. There we ate and shared how we were doing. We talked about our plans for the day before committing them to God in prayer.

Gerda received tremendous loving support and help from her oncologists and health-care practitioners at Joseph Brant Hospital and the Juravinski Cancer Centre. Throughout late spring and summer she was given radiation for her back, shoulder, and head, but while the tumours were shrinking, her overall condition was deteriorating.

Another significant event of that summer was our family photo shoot—pictures that have become treasures.

We had been talking as a family about doing a photo shoot for a while, but it looked like the earliest we could all get together would be the beginning of September. Then providentially, on the evening of July 18, 2019, with just one day's notice, my whole family gathered at LaSalle Park, in Burlington, overlooking Lake Ontario. Nya had returned early from an out-of-town trip, and everyone else was available, including our photographer Reid.

The photo session was great fun. The high energy and antics of our seven grandchildren generally kept us all alert, and this time was no exception. Gerda viewed times like these as "happy chaos."

It was a beautiful, warm, sunny evening. Following the family photo session, Reid and our son David took Gerda and me by ourselves down to the marina for pictures at the water's edge. Suddenly I had a vivid flashback to our wedding day. Almost thirty-eight years earlier we had stood embracing on the shores of the same lake with the sun setting behind us. The circle was closing the same way it had begun. I was in tears, realising we may well be ending married life the same way we started it, with photos by Lake Ontario in each other's arms.

These precious pictures reminded me of the many blessings we had experienced with each other and our family. They provided us with a great source of strength as we continued our journey through the valley of the shadow of death.

CHAPTER 17

The Valley of the Shadow of Death

Gerda continued to see God's love expressed in many ways, especially through Bible passages and the colour yellow. One day she asked, "Do you remember giving me flowers in 1976 when you first visited me at my parents' home?"

"Yes!" I said, "I remember." The moment instantly came to mind. I had bought them and, to my delight, smuggled them into her parents house without her noticing. This was quite an achievement, considering Gerda was always with me showing me the many sites and tourist attractions around Niagara-on-the-Lake and Niagara Falls. On the day I was returning home to England, I slipped into her bedroom and left them by her bedside—a surprise for her before getting ready for the night. Secretly, I was probably hoping they would bring her sweet dreams of me!

She asked me, "Do you remember what flowers they were?"

I thought for a few moments. "No."

She smiled. "They were carnations. And the colour?"

I was baffled. Sensing a set-up, I gave up. "I have absolutely no idea."

In a quiet and reflective voice, she said, "They were yellow…"

In my thoughts, I could finish her incomplete sentence: … *because even back then, God was showing his love toward me so he could remind me of it now.*

There it was: God's love mystically revealed to us from the beginning of our relationship. I felt a deep sense of amazement at seeing more of God's fingerprints on our lives and felt thankful for the comfort the memory imparted to Gerda.

That summer Gerda spent extra time meditating on Psalm 23 about God as the Good Shepherd who walks with us through the valley of the shadow of death. Subsequently, at her celebration of love, we played a brief video clip of Gerda reflecting on the truths in this passage where she said:

"I have seen God in the last six to seven months, first of all with perfect timing for treatment. I just had the sense that Germany was the place we had to go, but the last time I was in Germany I was really missing home and wondering how I had gotten to a foreign country in a foreign land. I was pretty bummed I couldn't be home for Mother's Day. But even though it was through adverse circumstances, God got me home the day before Mother's Day.

I was also able to be there for Liam and Julia's birthdays, Susan and Liz's birthday, my own birthday, and our wedding anniversary. All through that time, by God's grace, I was feeling fairly good because of the steroids I was on due to the brain radiation they had to do, so again, another not so nice thing, but bringing an outcome that helped me enjoy my family and my days.

Just the beauty of the tokens of love that came every single day was overwhelming. Now I know I have taken a turn for the worse, and it's not as easy to be as "up" as it was during those days, but these days are a really big blessing.

I think what I need everyone to know is that first of all, in the difficulties they may find in life, God is there to help, and he is willing to lead and guide to help us through them, and to grow us through them so we are not the same. I can tell you I am not the same woman I was in my twenties, thirties, or forties, or even fifties, and that he has continued to change my life in profound ways, most of all through some of the hard times.

He will never, ever, ever leave you…in good times or bad."

When David videoed this conversation with Gerda, we had no idea that twelve days later she would be "shepherded" through the doors of Carpenter House Hospice for a very special homegoing.

CHAPTER 18

It's Time to Go

From the time we took the family photos in the middle of July, Gerda's decline accelerated, and our focus was on managing pain and keeping her comfortable. By early August, we set up a hospital bed on the main floor of our house, enabling Gerda to spend her days downstairs, resting comfortably while enjoying visits with family and friends in our family room.

The last time she came downstairs from our bedroom was to celebrate Makayla's ninth birthday on Sunday, September 1. The next night, she could no longer keep her oral medications down, so the following day, they were administered through injections.

Gerda's desire, as well as mine and that of our family's, was for her to stay home and not go into a hospice or hospital unless absolutely necessary. This seemed very feasible since we had set up home health care. We had an amazing and competent team in place ready to help keep her in a home setting. Our daughter Susan, a trained nurse, was carefully overseeing everything, and Gerda's good friend Val, a former surgical assistant to a cardiovascular surgeon, was also providing wise counsel and support. At the same time, we wanted to know the steps we might need to take in case we found it necessary to move her to a health-care unit.

On Wednesday, September 4, Laurie Smith from Carpenter House came to meet with Gerda, me, and our children to explain the admissions process. This meeting was very positive in several ways. Laurie was the mother of Matt, one of our son David's good high school friends. After their joyful reunion, David explained how they knew each other. This common connection through Matt immediately gave us a bond, and it felt like we had a friend in the room and not a stranger.

Laurie explained the intake process and answered all our questions. She also informed us that a bed was currently available for Gerda, something that could not be guaranteed in the future. I thanked her and said we would let her know if and when we were ready for this next step.

With great wisdom Laurie turned to Gerda, who had been quietly listening to the conversation, and said, "And what do you think, Mama?"

The question caught me by surprise; I had thought our conversation was already over.

I was astonished when Gerda softly replied, "It's time to go!"

We all stood in shock, unprepared for her response. Liz, my daughter, was the first to collect herself and engage in dialogue. "Are you saying this because you think you will get better care than at home?"

"Yes," she quietly replied.

"Are you saying this because it will be easier on us?"

"Yes."

"Are you absolutely sure?"

"Yes."

I could see my sweetheart's confident resolve. Nothing was going to change her mind. Now was the time to go.

Gerda signed her own admission papers, and we immediately made arrangements for her to be moved the next day.

Later that afternoon, our family, along with our friend Charles Sathmary, gathered one more time to storm the gates of Heaven in prayer asking for Gerda's healing, knowing and believing that with God all things are possible.

In the evening Dr. Chris, one of Gerda's oncologists from Joseph Brant, stopped by to see how she was doing—a gesture of kindness well beyond her call of duty, and one I will never forget. She offered her love and support, and before leaving, gave me her personal phone number to call at any time during the night if we needed advice or help. The overnight nurse administered Gerda's medications, vigilantly sitting in a chair by her bed, doing everything possible she could to keep her as comfortable as possible. This arrangement allowed me, our three children, and Julia, our granddaughter, to sleep and be available as needed.

Before laying down beside Gerda to sleep, I spoke with her for the last time. We affirmed our love for one another, exchanged kisses, held hands, and committed the night to our loving heavenly Father. During the night she slipped into unconsciousness, never to wake again this side of Heaven.

The next morning, Thursday, September 5, the patient carriers, with the help of my children, very carefully carried her down the stairs and into the private ambulance. I joined her and Susan, who attentively monitored her condition on the two-kilometre route to Carpenter House. The driver, determined to give Gerda the smoothest possible ride, drove slowly and cautiously, while I, anxious to get there as soon as possible, stressed at the seemingly never-ending journey.

By 11:45 a.m., Gerda was warmly welcomed by the attentive nursing staff and made as comfortable as possible in her room. I relaxed, feeling a sense of relief that Gerda had made the right decision to go to Carpenter House. The corner room was bright and spacious, large enough to accommodate a good number of visitors at once and for me to sleep by her side, just as I planned. Across the hallway was a private gathering room where people could congregate and visit. It was a perfect setting in every way.

Gerda's brothers John and David, with their wives Susan and Gwyn, were already there to greet us when we arrived and they were the first to spend time with her. After their visit, David and Gwyn left to catch their flight home to New Brunswick. Then friends Bud and Beulah prayed with her before leaving to prepare for Bud's eye surgery that afternoon. What happened next was entirely spontaneous and very profound.

At first there were seven of us with Gerda, who remained unconscious: our children, Susan, Liz and David, daughter-in-law Mandy, friends Richard and Moira Brown, and me. Moira read to Gerda from the book *90 Minutes in Heaven* by Don Piper, the true story of a man who died and spent ninety minutes in Heaven.

As she finished reading, the senior pastor from our church, Paul Eastwood, arrived.

I greeted him at the door jokingly saying, "Hi Paul, welcome to 'The Service!' " As Paul and I walked toward Gerda, with me explaining what we were doing, another knock came. I returned to open the door, and there stood one of the hospice volunteers holding a vase of gorgeous yellow roses for Gerda. Excited, I accepted them and hurried to the foot of her bed to show her. "Honey! Honey, look at these beautiful yellow roses, just for you!"

After this flurry of activity, and with the flowers on a table to the side, Pastor Paul and Richard both read passages from the Psalms and prayed.

At that time, Glenda DeVries, another pastoral team member and close friend arrived, and I explained about "The

Service." Someone suggested we sing a hymn. We decided on, "How Great Thou Art," a favourite of Gerda's that we had sung at our wedding reception. Susan found a version on her iPhone that she knew her mother liked, and we all sang together.

As we reached the last line, my sweetheart took a big gasp of air. Susan calmly announced, "She has gone!"

"What do you mean, 'gone?' " I asked, as a hot flash of alarm shot through me. It was a reality I didn't want to accept. *She can't be dead! That's not possible!*

For one bizarre second, I expected Susan to reply, "No she is not dead."

Instead, she continued checking her vitals.

"She is gone," she said, and asked calmly, "What time is it?" I was behind Richard and saw over his shoulder that the face of his digital watch showed 4:04 p.m.

For a few moments, stunned silence descended on the room. I was in disbelief and shock. Totally dumbfounded!

Suddenly a scream and wail shattered the stillness. It was our daughter Liz. She ran to the bathroom retching violently, and I followed her, trying to bring her some consolation. We stood, rocking back and forth, holding each other in our arms, tears streaming down our faces. After a while, we rejoined everyone in the room. Liz then curled up with her mother on the bed.

Soon afterward, another of our church leaders, Pastor Doug, arrived. Now we were ten in number. When he heard the news, he expressed his condolences and disappointment at not having been there earlier. I appreciated his coming. Every bit of support we received was precious.

Someone later asked me, "Did you see the colour of Pastor Doug's shirt?" I hadn't noticed.

"It was yellow," they offered.

As our friends began to disperse, Val Crawford arrived, followed shortly by Dr. Witcher. She came not just to fulfil her duties as a doctor, but as a deeply caring healthcare provider who, through her vocation, had become a special friend to Gerda.

Susan, Val, and David placed some greenery and two yellow roses in Gerda's hands, which were resting on her midriff. It was a beautiful touch as they coordinated with the yellow pyjamas with a rose print she was wearing having put them on the previous evening due to being hot in everything else.

In many ways, the day was special, particularly because of the gift of having all those gathered around Gerda at the moment she left her earthly body. While I knew she wasn't doing well, I wasn't aware she was so close to the end. Later, I learned that Susan had been warning us it could happen soon, though she didn't know exactly when. For me, our three children, Mandy, our daughter-in-law, and other friends to be with her at the exact moment she passed away was extraordinary—even surreal.

As my family was together with Dr. Witcher and Val in the room, we reminisced about things that had taken place before they had arrived. A tangible peace lingered as we laughed, cried, and marvelled together. So penetrating was the peace that it overrode the raw heartache and emotions we were feeling, replacing them with quietness and calmness as we came to terms with the fact that Gerda's battle was over, and she was now safely in her new home.

Both David and I shared details of visions we had experienced. David was very clear about the timing of his vision concerning Gerda and talked about it at her celebration of life nine days later. As for mine, I have no idea when it happened or how—was it an impression, a dream or a thought? I feel safest calling it a vision, as I know I wasn't asleep at the time.

Eventually, while holding each other close, we entrusted Gerda's body to the care of the funeral directors.

My children came home with me for a *shawarma* meal David had ordered—our first meal of the day. Everyone helped tidy up around the house, and someone even made my bed with fresh, clean sheets. We dispersed. They went home to be with their families, and I lay in bed in a quiet, empty house for the first time since Gerda had attended Wesley Acres fourteen months earlier. This time, things were different. Gerda wouldn't be returning to share it with me.

It was a paradox. My heart was broken and grieving, yet all was well with my soul. By God's grace, I "slept like a baby" that night and every night since.

As I reflect on those four hours and nineteen minutes Gerda spent at Carpenter House—a very short time—I realise something "out of this world" took place through a precious and beautiful ceremony to prepare Gerda for Heaven. Had I been able to script what had transpired, I could never have come close to giving her such a triumphant transition to her new home. In that short time, she was:

- greeted by "angelic" staff and volunteers who attended to every detail to make her comfortable
- visited and surrounded by a room full of loving family and friends
- presented with an exquisite bouquet of yellow roses
- read a story about the beauty of Heaven
- encouraged with Scriptures that were so real to her
- offered prayer, words of affirmation, and love
- surrounded by a crowd of us singing her favourite hymn the moment she entered Heaven

I could imagine Gerda fully experiencing the truth of this verse, from How Great Thou Art, as we sang it at her bedside:

When Christ shall come
With shouts of acclamation
And take me home,
What joy shall fill my heart!

Then I shall bow
In humble adoration
And there proclaim,
My God, how great Thou art!

For a short while we are apart.

CHAPTER 19

Farewell, My Beloved

On Monday, September 9, 2019, we gathered with family and friends at Smith's Funeral Home, in Burlington, to say our final farewell to Gerda before escorting her body to its resting place.

The funeral director Don Smith and his team provided exceptional service and guided us through the process with no detail overlooked. Family and friends visited with Gerda before my family had some "alone time" with her.

Surprisingly, a good amount of joy and laughter was mixed with tears as we shared memories of things she had done and said. Makayla, Liam, Julia, and Kyleigh brought paintings and drawings they had made for her and lovingly placed them beside her in the coffin. After our last family photograph together, we hugged one another and prayed a prayer of thanksgiving for this amazing woman who had played such an irreplaceable part in our lives.

We held onto each other as we gazed one last time at Gerda's beautiful face before the casket was closed. She then started her final earthly journey to Burlington Memorial Gardens, a cemetery nestled under the Niagara Escarpment on the outskirts of the city.

It was perfect weather: a beautiful, warm, sunny, Ontario fall day with hardly a whisper of wind and just a scattering of fluffy white clouds in a vibrant blue sky. The burial was exactly how she had desired, quiet, without pomp and ceremony, and attended by her family and some close friends.

Among those attending were some special guests. Our nephews Alistair, Austin, and Andrew had all flown in from various parts of the United States. They, along with David and my son-in-law, Jordan, were the pallbearers, and helped me carry Gerda to the graveside. When her casket was in position, Bud Penner gave a short message of encouragement and an assurance of eternal life based on the Scripture John 14:1-4 (*NIV*) where Jesus said:

Do not let your hearts be troubled. You believe in God; believe also in me. My Father's house has many rooms; if that were not so, would I have told you that I am going there to prepare a place for you? And if I go and prepare a place for you, I will come back and take you to be with me so that you also may be where I am. You know the way to the place where I am going.

Such a comforting and strengthening truth!

After Glenda DeVries' prayer of thanksgiving and blessing, everyone was invited to lay a long-stemmed yellow rose on Gerda's elegant, light oak casket. The beautiful arrangement of roses remained in place as I lowered Gerda's coffin into the ground with the help of an electric winch.

As people were dispersing, our youngest grandchild Bennett, not quite two at the time, was holding a yellow rose head. He was supposed to drop it in the open grave, but instead he walked to each family member inviting them to sniff it. When he was done, he went back to the graveside and tossed it on top of Gerda's casket. It was a final, and unplanned, benediction from one of Gerda's most favourite little people.

I remember an overwhelming longing to stay by the graveside once everyone had gone. It was so strong that I had to peel myself away reluctantly knowing family and friends were waiting at our house. Now though, I wish I had stayed longer just to soak in the sense of closeness I felt with her at that moment. Today I am so thankful for this special quiet place where I can go to reflect on the incredible blessing it was to share life with such a woman of love and grace.

The burial day was a day filled with immense pain and loss, mingled with a mysterious aura of peace based on the knowledge that she was now in her eternal home. Two days later my family started preparing for Gerda's celebration of life. I renamed it a celebration of love because that's what it was—a story about love.

CHAPTER 20

Celebration of Love: The Setting

Five days after the funeral, we gathered at Compass Point Bible Church. Hundreds of people who loved and cared deeply for Gerda, me and our family were in attendance. The "words celebration of love" truly captured the essence of what I knew Gerda wanted us to communicate.

Just a few days before her passing she specifically said to me, "Don't make the celebration about me." I knew what she meant. She wanted it to be outwardly focused, but inevitably, she was "the star of the show," so it was impossible for her not to be front and centre for this event. As we prepared, one word surfaced in every communication: the word "love"! As a result, we titled the gathering A Love Story.

A huge arrangement of white and yellow balloons in the shape of a heart welcomed guests as they entered the church foyer. To access the sanctuary, people walked under a balloon archway creatively designed by Susan of Ettridges, The Studio Inc. The mood was celebratory.

In the auditorium, forming the backdrop on the platform, were yellow panels that cast a soft glow and drew the eye to an illuminated cross above. In front of the panels were four super-sized and evenly spaced letters that spelled the word "L O V E." Bouquets of helium-filled yellow balloons stood on either side.

A stunning yellow floral garland from our church graced the front edge of the podium, beautifully facing the auditorium. On either side of this centrepiece were plant arrangements that included one of Gerda's favourites: blue hydrangeas.

In honour of my precious bride I wore the black bow tie from our wedding with a white shirt and black suit. Family members, along with Bud and Beulah, joined me in a side room before we walked into the auditorium together. We all wore yellow corsages to remind us that while grieving our loss, we were also rejoicing at her induction into Heaven—a wonder that words cannot describe. *It's like being at a wedding feast,* I mused.

As we moved into the church foyer and prepared to enter the auditorium, the song "Jerusalem," by John Starnes, was playing. The music gave me a flashback of the first time my sweetheart and I drove into Jerusalem. That song was playing on the coach's sound system. I could still see Gerda singing along passionately, beaming with joy and excitement as the

Holy City came into view. The vivid memory jolted me and broke me emotionally, especially when I recalled her pointing out, with childlike glee, a white dove flying alongside the bus at exactly the same moment.

This rush of sentiment took me by surprise, and for a moment I thought, *Will I have the strength to move forward as the master of ceremonies and accomplish everything I've planned for the occasion?*

Suddenly, I was even more thankful Bud and Beaulah were part of our processional. I had planned to walk ahead of my family with both of them bringing up the rear, but my sudden wavering prompted me to ask them to walk beside me. What a difference it made! Their presence strengthened me for what lay ahead. Together with Bud and Beaulah I led my family into the sanctuary to the sound of John Denver's "Perhaps Love," a song that so well describes the power of love.

Perhaps love is like a resting place,
a shelter from the storm.
It exists to give you comfort.
It is there to keep you warm.
And in those times of trouble
when you are most alone,
the memory of love will bring you home.

When the family was seated I welcomed everyone who had joined us both in person and by livestream. Tributes followed. First Gerda's friend Theresa Vander Laan spoke followed by Gerda's brother John. We heard eulogies from our niece Kate on behalf of Gerda's other brother David and our three children. They all celebrated her love and genuineness. Makayla, representing the grandchildren, read these scriptures that so perfectly captured Gerda's essence:

Love is patient and kind.
Love does not envy or boast;
it is not arrogant or rude.
it does not insist on its own way;
it is not irritable or resentful;
it does not rejoice at wrongdoing,
but rejoices with the truth.
Love bears all things,
believes all things,
hopes all things,
endures all things.
Love never ends.
(1 Corinthians 13:4-8a, *ESV*)

I spoke briefly of the incredible privilege and honour of being Gerda's husband. She was a woman of beauty outwardly and inwardly. Her inner quietness and strength had shone through every aspect of her life and graced every relationship and situation. The Scripture I chose for the bulletin characterised her beautifully: *"Let it be the hidden person of the heart with the imperishable jewel of a gentle and quiet spirit, which in God's sight is very precious*" (I Peter 3:4, *RSV*).

Following the speeches, a slideshow of family photographs faded in and out to the words of our love song, Anne Murray's "Could I Have This Dance." Immediately after, seven of us who had been with Gerda when she passed away shared what transpired at that time. The first was David's account of his vivid vision of Heaven.

CHAPTER 21

Celebration of Love: Matthew

On the stage were our children Susan, Liz, and David, daughter-in-law Mandy, friend Moira Brown, Pastor Paul Eastwood, and I.

"We have a beautiful family story to share," Liz said as she introduced this segment of the program.

"First, we'd like to start with two background stories." David's wife, Mandy, then shared her experience from nearly four years earlier when she was expecting their second baby.

One night, during Mandy's first trimester, she had a dream that she miscarried. In the dream she was holding a baby boy in the palm of her hand. The pre-term baby appeared completely at peace, calm, and safe. She was filled with much joy because God had given them a baby boy. She was excited to tell David, *It's a boy! It's a boy!* She had no sense of sadness, hurt, or anger.

Immediately after the dream, in the middle of the night, she woke up and miscarried. She and David realised the dream had been a gift from God that allowed them to know they had a child in Heaven, a baby boy. They decided to name their baby Matthew, meaning "gift from God."

Then Liz told Gerda's story of asking God to remind her of his love through the colour yellow.

Susan spoke of how she had seen God in every detail of our journey, even in the things that were sad or painful. Before she and her family had come to Germany to visit us, they had memorised certain Scriptures to help them focus on the importance of listening to God, trusting him, and knowing he would never leave them alone.

Moira read the section from Don Piper's book *90 Minutes in Heaven* that she had shared at Carpenter House.

Paul read a meditation from Psalm 121 that asks, *"From where does our help come?"* It was very timely and appropriate to our situation. The answer in the next verse says it comes from *"the Lord, maker of Heaven and Earth."*

We told everyone about the special delivery of the yellow roses and of singing "How Great Thou Art" as she passed away just prior to the arrival of Pastor Doug in his yellow shirt.

Then David spoke. He told a story of what happened the day before she passed away when our family, along with Pastor Charles Sathmary, were praying with her in our bedroom.

David remembered that when he was afraid as a child, his mother taught him from Psalm 23 that God is the Good Shepherd who "makes us lie down in green pastures," even when the going gets tough in dark and scary times. That day, at Gerda's bedside, he silently prayed this Psalm over his mother.

He also mentioned his disappointment that at his Oma's (grandmother's) passing nine months earlier, both his sisters had seen a vision of her in Heaven, but he had not. He felt left out. He asked God, "If Mom goes, will you please give me a vision of her in Heaven?"

Amazingly, as he prayed, he suddenly received a two-frame vision. In the first frame Gerda was lying on green grass, so peacefully. In the second, she got up and looked right at him with the greatest joy he had ever seen on anyone's face.

The following day at the hospice, during our impromptu "Service," while we were singing the chorus to "How Great Thou Art," the vision returned—this time with four frames. Once again, his mother was lying on the green grass. Then standing up, she looked directly at him with immense joy, singing the words to "How Great Thou Art" at the top of her lungs. Suddenly she stopped singing, turned around, and started running through the green grass chasing a little boy. David knew immediately it was his son Matthew.

Later I asked David for a word that described his feelings at that time.

“There isn’t a word in the English language,” he said. “It was peace, delightful. I was taken aback. That’s my son? No way! Mom’s got a grandchild in Heaven! He’s grown? I want to hold him!”

The vision brought such great comfort and joy to David and Mandy. Just the evening before, David had said to Gerda how happy he was that she would soon see Matthew. Now they knew Gerda had not only seen him but was also playing with him. One of her favourite pastimes on Earth had been playing with her precious grandchildren.

CHAPTER 22

Celebration of Love: Gerda's Special Message

The guest of honour at the celebration of love was Gerda herself. Toward the end of the ceremony we showed a segment from the video David had taped of her just twelve days before her passing. She spoke from experience about the reality of facing eternity.

"It's interesting to live through Psalm 23, which is what you do when you experience something like this." She quoted the Psalm: *"Even though I walk through the valley of the shadow of death, I will fear no evil for you are with me,'* " and continued:

"Jesus is described as a shepherd here, who walks through the valley with you—a shepherd who takes care of his sheep. A shepherd who has a rod to ward off whatever evil tries to get at you and a staff to keep you safe because the road is not easy. You may slip and fall, or digress and take detours, but the staff…brings you back to him. He is very faithful to do that. It's interesting. Here he's the shepherd walking with you, not the King of Kings and Lord of Lords…, which is also who he is. But in these moments, he's not Lord of Hosts or God Almighty or the King of Glory, even though he is all these things. When he walks through the valley of the shadow of death with you, he is the shepherd who is looking after you."

Gerda shared how at fourteen she attended Eden Christian High School in Niagara-on-the-Lake. During October of her first year, they had Bible Emphasis Week when they taught biblical truths and challenged the students about their personal relationship with Christ. Gerda identified this as a pivotal time in her spiritual life, saying:

"I had gone to church all my life and knew all the Bible stories: Jonah and the big fish, Daniel in the lions' den, David and Goliath. I knew all those stories really well, but I never understood about Easter. I didn't understand why Jesus had to come. I didn't understand why he had to die on a cross. I didn't know why we celebrated his resurrection.

So, during this week, I realised that Jesus had come for the express purpose of dying for my sins—the things I had done wrong—and everyone else's as well. I needed to ask his forgiveness for those sins and to ask him to come into my life so I can have a relationship with him."

Gerda talked about how one night during that week she had knelt by her bed and asked Jesus to come into her "heart" and to forgive her of all her sins, but nothing out of the ordinary happened. She added:

"I didn't hear a voice from Heaven. I didn't get a special feeling. There wasn't...a sudden flow of peace.... Nothing happened! I just made that decision based on the message I had heard, [this message] I thought was the most important one I had ever heard in my life. And that is when I began my relationship with Jesus that has lasted all these years."

She quoted Jesus' words that meant so much to her: *"For God so loved the world that he gave his one and only Son, that whoever believes in him shall not perish, but have eternal life. For God did not send his Son into the world to condemn the world, but to save the world through him"* (John 3:16-17, *NIV*).

John 11:25 tells the story of Lazarus who died and Martha, Lazarus's sister, said to Jesus, *"Lord, if you had been there, he wouldn't have died."* Jesus responded: *"I am the resurrection and the life. Whoever believes in me, though he dies, yet shall he live. and everyone who lives and believes in me shall never die. Do you believe this?"*

In recounting this story to David, Gerda affirmed: "I believe [the same thing] one hundred percent, from the bottom of my heart, and my response is the same as Martha's: Yes, Lord, I believe you are the Christ, the Son of the living God who is to come into the world."

About eight years prior to Gerda's passing we read the book *Heaven is for Real.* An amazing and miraculous story of a boy named Colton Burpo, who at three years and ten months almost died during emergency surgery, went to Heaven, and returned to tell the story. Little by little, Colton unfolded what had happened during his time in Heaven. He revealed impossible things he couldn't have known, like details of what people were doing during the surgery. Colton talked about the people he met in Heaven, including his sister who had been miscarried before he was born, something he had never been told.

The reality of Heaven was very comforting to both of us during Gerda's illness and even more so to me afterward. With the knowledge that Heaven is real, Gerda shared her heart.

"We must think about our eternity. We can't just think this life is the only [life] there is. There is a life beyond, and we need to be ready for it. That means beginning a relationship with Christ here on Earth.... The invitation I'd like to give to everyone is to give him a chance. Ask him if he is real. Ask him if he loves you. Ask him to show himself to you. Give him a chance without writing him off as one who's not important or...a myth, or for people who need a crutch. He makes the difference between life here and life in eternity, and I want people to give him a chance."

This was Gerda's testimony and invitation for us all to continue on our journey toward intimacy with God.

CHAPTER 23

Celebration of Love: The Invitation

I both appreciate and dislike attending funerals and celebrations of life. I like them because they bring back fond memories of the one who passed, and deepen my appreciation for them through stories shared by friends and family. I dislike them because they often stir up feelings of grief and sorrow.

As master of ceremonies for Gerda's celebration of love, by God's grace, I completed my assignments as planned, even though I experienced the impact of grief and loss more that day than at any other such event. Thankfully, I was able to release most of my emotional heartache while seated at the front of the church in the dark, rather than in the spotlight while standing behind the microphone. Many times tears streamed down my face until it was time to go forward again. I am grateful to Bud for being by my side and gently resting his hand on my shoulder. His touch gave me strength, inspiring me to carry on.

Gerda spoke of giving God a chance. As the celebration drew to a close, I offered information and resources that people might find helpful in their continued walk toward a personal relationship with God.

I referenced the book and movie *90 Minutes in Heaven* and shared my own story of how my life was disrupted by factual evidence supporting Jesus's resurrection. The author of the book and movie *The Case for Christ*, on a similar vein, gives his account. It is the true story of Lee Strobel, an atheist and investigative journalist who discovered undeniable, hard facts that supported the biblical claims of Jesus's birth, death, and resurrection.

Above all, I wanted everyone to know that God is love, and in him there is rest for our souls. I quoted Jesus when he said: *"Come to me all who are weary and are burdened, and I will give you rest. Take my yoke upon you and learn from me; for I am gentle and humble in heart, and you will find rest for your souls. For my yoke is easy, and my burden is light"* (Matthew 11:28-30, *RSV*).

As people left that day, we gave away one hundred copies of *Heaven is for Real* and invited them to join an Alpha course that would begin soon at our church. Alpha is a series of open, friendly discussions about Jesus's purpose and relevance to life.

Finally I invited guests to join our family in the foyer for refreshments and visit a small display of family memorabilia, photographs, and three of Gerda's keepsake items for people to view.

The first of these keepsakes, on the wall behind the display, was Janice Cameron's handcrafted, beautiful patchwork quilt that Gerda had kept close to her for nine months.

The second was a print my brother Neil gave to Gerda and me for our wedding. It is a picture of a typical northern England farm built in the 1600s with barns clustered around the farmhouse and fences clearly marking the fields on the hillside behind it. Everything—including houses, buildings and field fences—was made of stone, the primary building material used in that region at the time.

This print meant a lot to me because it reminded me of the farms where I was raised, but during Gerda's final months, it came to mean much more to her than it had previously. In the picture an elderly shepherd is leaving the farmyard with his two border collies, which are herding a small flock of Swaledale sheep. If you look carefully, you see the shepherd is cradling a small lamb in his arms. The image reflected Gerda's unwavering confidence that God was her good shepherd holding her securely in his loving arms.

This watercolour by Alan Ingham, titled "Down from the Hills," depicted Gerda's feeling of safety and shelter from the storms of life. We had it re-matted and framed after we returned from Germany so it could hang on the wall in our family room where we spent most of our time.

The third was an item my daughter found in our basement storage just a few days before the celebration of love: our wedding program. I had forgotten it existed. She showed it to me excitedly. It was a stock wedding bulletin we had chosen for our order of service. The cover caption read, *"Love is of God"* (1 John 4:7, *RSV*), and next to it was the image of a *single yellow rose!*

As each person left the auditorium, we gave them a yellow rose, a copy of the Gospel of John titled, *So Loved*, and a bookmark titled, "You Are Loved" with these words on it:

Love is invincible facing danger and death.
Passion laughs at the terrors of hell.
The fire of love stops at nothing—
it sweeps everything before it.
Flood waters can't drown love;
torrents of rain can't put it out.
Love can't be bought; love can't be sold.
(Song of Solomon, 8:6–7, *MSG*)

With the passage of time, I have come to understand more fully how all along God had been reaching out in love saying: *We can do all things together. Just hold my hand.*

Scan to watch: The Celebration of Love

TThe flowers I sent to Gerda at Wesley Acres Retreat Centre, before I knew she had chosen the colour yellow to remind her of God's love for her..

Walking through the gardens in Bad Salzhausen, Germany, ablaze with the colour yellow.

Family photograph, August 18, 2019.

Our last walk together on Lake Ontario.

PART III

CHAPTER 24

"Hold My Hand; We Will Walk in the Sand"

Our en-suite bathroom reflects a beach theme, decorated with pictures and cherished items we've collected over the years that remind us of our countless visits to the ocean. Amongst them is a wall plaque. If I could bring Gerda back for just one day and do anything I chose with her, I would use the words on that plaque and say, "Hold my hand; we will walk in the sand."

During our honeymoon in Rockport we realised how much we loved being with each other by the sea. It gave us our first taste of life together at the ocean, and our appetite for it only intensified. As a result, we visited many beautiful seaside places and walked the beaches with their ever-changing landscapes of sandbars and wading pools that appeared and disappeared overnight.

Gerda was carefree and energised by the ocean. It always filled her with excitement and brought out the little girl in her, whether along the surf's edge in North Carolina where warm, salty water lapped at her ankles, or while bracing against the cool winds of Scotland's shore in the Outer Hebrides and Mull of Kintyre where my father grew up. Our walks along the cold, windswept beaches of Scotland became one of our most treasured souvenirs of our twenty-fifth wedding anniversary we celebrated there.

For more than fifteen years, we vacationed with Bud and Beulah and other good friends in North Myrtle Beach. Our accommodations overlooked pristine beaches that stretched sixty miles along the Atlantic Ocean.

We walked along the water's edge side by side, hand in hand, feeling the waves wash over our toes and quickly erode the sand beneath them. Ah! A bit of Heaven on Earth! My dear Gerda loved endlessly searching for seashells, reading books on the beach, playing bocce ball in the sand, and feeling the sea breeze against her face and in her hair. She watched the sunrise across the water, searched for dolphins, and gazed into the star-filled sky identifying constellations, all the while marvelling at the vastness and beauty of our world. It refreshed her soul, and she couldn't wait to return each year.

Memories! Glorious days in our lives that are so precious! The days of walks with my sweetheart are over, and that chapter is closed. I now hold no one's hand, and only my footprints remain in the sand.

Sand and footprints remind me of a popular poem called "Footprints in the Sand," that describes a man's dream in which he is walking along a beach with the Lord. In the dream, he reflects upon his life and sees two sets of footprints, one belonging to him and the other to the Lord. The man contemplates various scenes from the dream and becomes confused when he notices that at times, instead of there being two sets of footprints, there is only one. He realizes the one set of footprints appeared at the most difficult times of his life. Baffled by the revelation, he asks, "Lord, I don't understand why, when I needed you the most, you were not there for me." The Lord whispers, "My dear child, those are the times I carried you in my arms."

Like this man, I couldn't see God at work during my difficult seasons. But as I took time to reflect, I discovered treasures hidden in these dark places, just as the Scripture promises:

"I will give you treasures hidden in the darkness—
secret riches,
I will do this so you may know that I am the LORD,
the God of Israel, the one who calls you by name."
(Isaiah 45:3,NLT).

CHAPTER 25

Tapestry

Several years have passed since I lost my beautiful wife, and they have been years of profound reflection.

I have experienced a depth of emotions, feelings, and insights I didn't know I was capable of having.

I have re-lived the joy of many wonderful memories: our meeting, our life together, our beautiful children, and our delightful grandchildren.

I have grieved and missed Gerda as I reflected on special occasions we would have attended together.

I deeply regret the many mistakes I made and wish I had been a better friend and husband to Gerda. I only wish I had corrected my wayward thoughts and actions more swiftly.

I miss more than ever her elegance and sheer beauty, and above all, her gracious heart, gentle and quiet spirit that only sought to love and do good.

I grieve because she is not there to greet me when I come home, and my heart aches to feel her gentle touch, kisses, and caresses.

I weep because I cannot experience my most favourite time of day any longer—falling asleep in her arms.

I miss her in so many ways.

These memories and the emotions they stir remind me of a story called *The Hiding Place*.

Between 1938 and 1945, our world was in turmoil with millions suffering horribly due to World War II. Among them, Corrie Ten Boom, her father, and sister were betrayed by a fellow Dutch citizen. They were arrested for hiding Jews from the Nazis and subsequently taken into captivity. Corrie's father died days later, but Corrie and her sister Betsie were taken to the notorious Ravensbruck Concentration Camp. Betsie died in the camp, while Corrie miraculously survived.

After the war Corrie travelled the world telling people "there is no pit so deep that God's love is not deeper still" and "God will give us the love to be able to forgive our enemies, just as Jesus did." Corrie often quoted the poem *Life is but a Weaving*.

My life is but a weaving
Between my God and me.
I cannot choose the colours
He weaveth steadily.

Oft' times he weaveth sorrow;
And I in foolish pride
Forget he sees the upper
And I the underside.

Not 'till the loom is silent
And the shuttles cease to fly
Will God unroll the canvas
And reveal the reason why.

The dark threads are as needful
In the weaver's skilful hand
As the threads of gold and silver
In the pattern he has planned.

He knows, he loves, he cares;
Nothing this truth can dim.
He gives the very best to those
Who leaves the choice to Him.

During my time of reflection, I have come to deeply appreciate the comparison of life to a beautiful tapestry, intricately and perfectly designed. On the front is a breathtaking, glorious masterpiece—carefully woven—while underneath it can seem messy with knots and loose hanging threads. The underside would represent the pain, disorder, and confusion we so often experience in life, while not realising the splendour of the image developing on the upper side. Occasionally, we catch a glimpse of the beauty of what is being created and stand in awe, noticing priceless treasures intricately woven into the design. That is precisely what happened to me when I uncovered certain patterns in my life.

CHAPTER 26

Circles of Life

In 1979, the first Christmas after we began our courtship, I scraped together as much money as possible to buy Gerda a gift. I wanted it to be something very special, believing it to be the first of many Christmases we would celebrate together. After much deliberation I purchased a delicate gold bracelet.

Fourty years later, three months after her passing, I faced my first Christmas without her, and the thought of my sweetheart not being there at that very special time of year was heartbreaking.

In the past, whenever Gerda asked me what I wanted for Christmas, I often said, "You are all I ever want. Just wrap yourself up and be under the tree!"

This sentiment was expressed in one of the cards I gave her on our last Christmas together:

My very favourite gift was never stashed beneath the tree.
It wasn't wrapped with ribbon, though it came
dressed beautifully.
There wasn't any curious box to shake to make a guess,
but I can still get all shook up,
I'm happy to confess, my very favourite gift is you!
You fill my life with love!
No wonder I feel blessed each day
And thank the Lord above!
Love you at Christmas and always!

I added words that reflected the deepest expression of my own heart: "No truer words have been written. You are all I have ever wanted for Christmas, and you will always be my favourite gift. Gerda, you are a treasure money cannot buy. I love you with all my heart. All my love, Ian." I signed off with four kisses and two smiley faces.

As Christmas approached, I started noticing an advertisement on Instagram© for a gold bracelet called "A forever diamond bangle." It was not the bling that caught my attention, but the words engraved on the inside of the band. They expressed my deepest thoughts and feelings. Every time I saw the commercial, I had a crazy idea of buying it for Gerda for Christmas. Eventually, I went ahead and ordered it, wondering how I should give it to her.

Each Christmas morning, before getting out of bed and starting the festivities with our family, Gerda and I used to have a special time together sharing Christmas cards and small gifts. Later in the day, with my family, we also had something under the tree for each other. Without Gerda, what would the day be like this year? How could I give her this symbolic gift without her being there? Would I do it quietly by myself in the bedroom as we usually did? I just didn't know.

Before I had devised a game plan, Lucille Mataos, one of Gerda's friends, bounced up to me at church one Sunday morning and out of the blue said, "Why don't you buy Gerda a Christmas present?" She asked me this so matter-of-factly, as if it was the most natural thing on earth to buy a deceased person a gift. I was surprised, because I hadn't mentioned the gift idea to anyone, but I found her words encouraging. Maybe buying a gift for Gerda wasn't so "crazy" after all. If Lucille thought it was a good idea, at least now I had good company.

"Well, actually," I began, gathering my thoughts, "I have already bought Gerda a gift, and I'm waiting for it to be delivered."

Without missing a beat, in classic, straightforward "Lucille style" she said, "Why don't you get your grandchildren to open it for her?"

"Okay, I'll think about that," I said, but thought, "*Wow! That sounds like a great idea,* without letting on what a big question it had been in my mind. I hoped my words had carried appropriate resolve.

On Christmas Day, when all other presents were unwrapped, I asked the grandchildren if anyone would like to open a special last gift for Grandma. I got a few looks of disbelief, as if they didn't think I could possibly be serious, but then they noticed one last small gift under the tree. The younger grandkids were more than eager to participate.

The day had been an emotional rollercoaster for all of us, filled with a bittersweet mixture of laughter and tears. We shared memories from the past about Gerda and revelled in the energy and excitement of the children as they opened their gifts. But it was different. We felt Gerda's absence.

Now all eyes were on the very last gift.

Makayla read the gift tag: "To my forever sweetheart, Gerda. All my love, now and forever." I signed my name with four kisses and two smiley faces.

Several of the grandchildren eagerly crowded around the gift, and with many helping hands, it was quickly opened. The bracelet was carefully lifted out. After everyone oohed and awed at the gold bracelet encrusted with sparkling faux-diamonds, I said, "There's an inscription inside the band." Through a blur of tears and gut-wrenching heartache, I read the simple words:

I loved you then,
I love you still.
I always have,
I always will.

I suddenly saw it clearly. It was a full circle moment. Two bracelets. For forty years, God's fingerprints had been on every detail of our lives, weaving a pattern in the tapestry, creating a beginning and an end, a first and last. The first bracelet anticipated a bright future on Earth; the last celebrated a glorious future together in Heaven.

Then I saw even more patterns. The tapestry was rich with them. They formed stories representing God's loving guidance throughout our lives. This is exactly why we told the stories at Gerda's celebration of love.

Immediately following the celebration, I said to my family, "Someone needs to write a book to tell this story." Given how much more gifted they were at telling stories than I, I fully expected one of them to quickly rise to the challenge. Instead, they all stared at me like deer caught in the headlights. Several days later, to my utter shock and bewilderment, I realised I was the one to do it.

I began writing our story eleven days after Gerda's celebration of love, while I was on a driving adventure I called, "A Journey of Remembrance and Thanksgiving." I didn't follow a detailed travel plan; I simply had a general idea of where I would go, visiting family, friends, and places that held special meaning for us both.

First, I travelled north to cottage country and then pointed my car east through to Canada's Maritime provinces. From there, I turned south toward the United States and New

England, including Pennsylvania and the Carolinas, before returning home three weeks later.

I spent the first night with friends Dan and Cindy Nicholson in Muskoka. This region is renown for its stunning natural beauty, especially its pristine lakes, dense forest, and rocky landscape. It is southern Ontario's premier cottage country equivalent to England's Lake District, without the mountains and hair-raising twisty, narrow roads.

Located in the heart of Muskoka, at the hub of the three largest lakes in the area, Muskoka, Joseph, and Rosseau, is the charming village of Port Carling. Dan and Cindy own a gorgeous home there with a beautiful view of Lake Muskoka. I woke up early the next morning and took advantage of the morning stillness to sit alone outside and absorb the quietness and magnificent beauty of the lake, but suddenly I had a flashback.

On my first visit to Canada in 1976 I met my friend Mark at the Toronto Airport.

We began our North American adventure by hitch-hiking out of this busy international airport—in hindsight, it is safe to say that this was probably not the smartest idea.

It was late in the day, and we only managed to travel a dismal two miles. As darkness fell, we set up camp by the Carling O'Keefe brewery (now Molson Coors) at the junction of Canada's busiest highway intersection, the 427 and 401. To minimise the chance of being detected, we found a secluded corner in the brewery's field by the highway, unrolled our tent, and without pitching it, crawled between the groundsheet and outer shell.

The next morning, we were up at the first hint of dawn, packed and prepared to risk our lives crossing ten lanes of 401 Highway traffic to continue our hitchhiking expedition. Fortunately, we got a couple of quick rides that swiftly took us out of the hustle and bustle of Toronto. The last driver dropped us off at the Lloydtown/Aurora exit on HWY 400, just north of Toronto, close to the small community of Kettleby.

Since it was still early on a Sunday morning and only a few cars were occasionally passing by, we decided to attend a service at a nearby church. As we walked along the footpath towards the traditional-looking church in this clearly upscale community, a smartly dressed lady approached and asked what we were doing. Given our appearance—unshaven, with shoulder length hair, wearing jeans and rumpled T-shirts, and carrying huge backpacks—her question was entirely reasonable.

She introduced herself as Jackie Catto, and we shared our hitch-hiking adventures and how we had landed on the doorstep of her church. Without hesitation, she said, "After the service, I'll be heading to our family cottage in the same direction you're going. Would you like a ride?" It felt like a dream come true, and we couldn't refuse. Immediately following the service, we went to Jackie's home to help her pack her station wagon with summer supplies for the cottage.

As we travelled together and got to know one other, she extended another invitation: "Would you like to spend the evening with me and my family at the cottage?" With no plans and no idea where we would stay the night, we gratefully accepted her gracious offer.

Along the way, Jackie had another surprise for us. She introduced us to the iconic Weber's Burgers, north of Orillia, and treated us to our first Canadian burger and fries. The memory of eating the mouth-watering, charcoal-grilled patties in buns within the unique railroad-themed setting has made it one of my favourite places to visit when I'm in that area.

An hour later we arrived at the Catto's family waterfront summer retreat, featuring two traditional Muskoka cottages, each two stories high and finished in white clapboard with dark green trim. Under the tall pines, the tranquil sound of water lapped gently at the shoreline with a soothing rhythm, creating a dreamy peace.

Their cottages were surrounded by lush greenery and towering evergreens right on the edge of beautiful Lake Rosseau.

We savoured the peaceful surroundings and the warm hospitality of our hosts Jackie, her children Lynda and Geoff, and her in-laws Mr. and Mrs Catto. Lynda and Geoff were a few years younger than us, but to ensure we fully experienced cottage life, they took us boating, played shuffleboard and tennis with us, and showed us around Port Carling.

Our initial one-night stay turned into two, and two into three, with an invitation to stay as long as we liked, but our plans to get to my sister's in Minneapolis forced us to move on. We eventually peeled ourselves away from this fairy tale setting where we were treated like royalty.

To this day, Jackie remains one of my precious friends.

This unexpected memory suddenly stirred my emotions deeply. I saw before me a circle of life. Dan and Cindy's home was very near Jackie's family cottage. It was another beginning and end; first and last; alpha and omega.

The trip in 1976 had been the catalyst for my life's adventure with Gerda, and here I was again in Port Carling embarking on a very different journey—one without her; a journey I would never have willingly chosen.

These memories and reflections brought a rush of painful heartache, but at the same time, I sensed comfort and peace in recognising this circle of life, and felt God say, "As I was with you on the adventure with Gerda, I will be with you on the adventure without her."

Since that day with Dan and Cindy, I have spent much time reflecting on the past. My contemplations revived other significant memories, like those of two meaningful physical touches I experienced with Gerda.

The first was in 1978, on the docks, as we parted ways at the end of her visit to Southampton, the day after I told her I didn't believe she was the right one for me. The memory of that sweet embrace on the docks before she boarded the ferry to France felt so right—as if we belonged in each other's arms. The second occurred just a few days prior to her passing.

Usually when we went to bed we embraced each other, thanked God for his blessings, and asked for protection over ourselves and our loved ones. We kissed and exchanged "I love you" before falling asleep, wrapped in each other's arms. We continued this tradition throughout Gerda's illness, adjusting as needed to accommodate her situation.

On that particular night, as I leaned in to kiss my sweetheart goodnight, our lips met in a uniquely special way. Unlike other evenings, we shared a passionate, lingering kiss. After exchanging our usual "I love you's," I lay down beside her and held her hand, and then she started tenderly caressing my hand—that was also unusual. A thought crossed my mind: *What's this all about?* At the time, I didn't realise we were so close to closing another circle of life.

A few days later she passed away. The beginning was a sweet embrace in 1978 saying, *Goodbye for now; we will soon be together for life.* The ending was a passionate farewell kiss and a gentle caress of my hand that was saying, *Goodbye for now; we will soon be together for eternity.*

To date I have identified six circles of life:

- The first and last Christmas gifts of bracelets.
- Our first and last marriage photographs together at the edge of Lake Ontario.

- "How Great Thou Art" sung the day our marriage began and the day it ended.
- The first and last flowers I gave her were both yellow.
- Port Carling, where I started my journey to find Gerda and my journey to release her.
- Our first and last meaningful touches that said we belong together for life and eternity.

These circles of life with my sweetheart are now closed. The Book of Ecclesiastes has a collection of sayings that have helped me put them into perspective:

For everything there is a season, and a time for every matter under Heaven: a time to be born, and a time to die…, a time to weep, and a time to laugh…, a time to mourn, and a time to dance; a time to love…, and a time for peace…. He has made everything beautiful in its time…. He has put eternity into man's heart. *(Ecclesiastes 3:1-11,* ESV*)*

And now it is a time to dance….

CHAPTER 27

A Time to Dance

My sweetheart loved to dance. One of her passions was waltzing, a love she developed during her German Mennonite upbringing. She loved dancing at family parties in homes, attending Oktoberfest-style events in the area where she lived, and while working in Germany every summer during her university years. She talked longingly about these special occasions, especially at Brock University when she waltzed and danced the polka with her German professor Dr. Schutz, a very accomplished dancer.

Sadly, she reflected on those events only as special memories. I couldn't be part of her dance. I had no sense of rhythm, and even with dance lessons, was never able to waltz with any reasonable level of competence. Yet we shared one special song, "Could I Have This Dance," by Canadian singer Anne Murray. We would slow-dance to it at weddings and on other special occasions. As we swayed to the music, holding each other close, we whispered in each others ears the words of the chorus:

Could I have this dance for the rest of my life?
Would you be my partner every night?
When we are together it feels so right.
Could I have this dance for the rest of my life?

When Gerda passed away, I had a vivid vision. I don't recall exactly when it came, but I shared it with my family at Carpenter House after she died, so it likely occurred around that time. I called it "The Last Waltz."

In the vision, Gerda and I were dancing a waltz with a proficiency well above my abilities. Suddenly, out of nowhere, Prince Charming appeared—sophisticated and captivating. He tapped me on my shoulder and, gliding effortlessly between us without looking at my face, said, "For thirty-eight years I gave her to you to dance with. Now it's my turn."

My sweetheart slipped out of my arms into his. With much heartache, I knew I had to release her.

Off they went, gliding effortlessly across the room, perfectly in sync with each other and in harmony with the music. Gerda smiled as she lovingly glanced back at me, and I could see how truly happy she was. I knew in that moment her longing had been fulfilled. She was in the arms of Jesus, whom she loved and adored with all her heart. Now, she was dancing the waltz of her life with him.

A few days after the celebration of love, I found a sealed envelope in a drawer where we kept a selection of unused greeting cards. The envelope was entirely out of place. I had never seen it before. I was surprised to see Gerda's writing on it. It simply said, "To Jesus." That evening, I gathered my family so we could open it together.

The note was dated July 19, 2010, a little more than nine years prior. In the letter Gerda explained that Beth Moore, one of her favourite Bible teachers, had challenged her to write a letter to Jesus, and be completely honest about her heart's desire. It was a brief letter covering a handful of her desires relating to various topics and relationships.

Halfway through the letter she wrote, "Oh, Lord, I want to feel and I want to dance! To waltz! To polka! To fly through a room, light on my feet, caught up in the music and sheer thrill of moving to it. I want to dance!"

The vision showed me the fulfilment of her heart's desire to "fly through a room" and dance with the one she so loved, the one who first loved her.

A [illegible] my sister. The celebration of love. I found a small sweater and drawer [illegible] a collection of unused greeting cards. The envelope was conspicuously out of place. I'd never seen it before. I was surprised to see Gertie's writing on it, a [illegible] card. "To Jesus." That evening, I read it to my family so we could grieve together.

The note was dated July 15, 2019, a little more than nine days prior to the [illegible] Gertie explained that [illegible] and [illegible] reminded me to write a letter to Jesus, and [illegible] about her [illegible] handled [illegible] desires relating to [illegible] related to us.

I believe [illegible] letter [illegible] and I want to dance. To walk? To [illegible] light on my feet [illegible] moving [illegible].

[illegible] showed me the fulfillment of her [illegible] desire [illegible] and [illegible] love.

The [illegible] loved her.

CHAPTER 28

Radical Love

Both Gerda and I experienced a radical, transformational love that illuminated our path through life, even during our darkest moments, filling us with the fullness of joy and a profound sense of gratitude.

Let me share a paraphrase—my own brief retelling of the most extraordinary story of radical love ever told. It is inexplicable, complex, and mystifying, yet at the same time simple, easy to understand, and filled with hope and purpose—truly profound.

A young woman conceived out of wedlock. It was a very unacceptable situation in her culture and time period, especially with her bizarre claim that she had become pregnant through a supernatural visitation. Her parents loved her and feared social ridicule and fatal consequences, especially since her fiancé denied being the father.

Her fiancé himself struggled to know how to deal with the betrayal and shame it brought on him and his family. In despair, he contemplated what action to take. The decision was in his power. Should he report her to the local judicial authorities for apparent unfaithfulness? If he did, he would be sentencing her to death. She would be stoned. That was the cultural punishment for marital unfaithfulness. But being the good man he was, who cared deeply for his fiancé, he decided against taking legal action and chose instead to end the relationship quietly.

While he was struggling with this question, one night an angel visited the man in a dream and told him that his fiancé was indeed telling the truth. He must marry her. The angel also revealed the name they were to give the baby boy and said the child was destined to fulfil a unique purpose that only he could accomplish.

Convinced the dream was a divine message, he believed and chose to marry his fiancé despite the mocking, scorn, and rejection he anticipated would be heaped on him.

The young woman left town immediately to visit an aunt in another village. It turned out this aunt was also pregnant under supernatural circumstances. She was well beyond childbearing age, but the baby she was expecting had also been prophesied by an angel who had appeared to her husband. As a result, her aunt recognised and accepted the supernatural element of the young woman's pregnancy.

The young woman stayed with her aunt for three months, and the two spent precious time together awaiting the arrival of their babies. They encouraged one another and marvelled at their extraordinary circumstances.

When the young woman's baby was due, a census was to be taken in their country. The couple travelled to their ancestral hometown to be registered. As expected, the town was overcrowded, and unfortunately overnight accommodations were unavailable. Eventually, they were offered a shelter used for farm livestock. The outbuilding was exposed to the elements and far from ideal for sleeping, but it was better than an open field. They gratefully accepted.

Had they tried to sleep, their sleep likely would have been short. That night, under a starlit sky, their baby boy arrived. Shortly after, nomadic shepherds belonging to the lowest social cast appeared, seeking to honour the baby. They shared a remarkable story of how, while they were tending sheep on the hillsides surrounding the town, angels appeared in the sky instructing them to find this special newborn baby. The parents marvelled and treasured the moment in their hearts.

Sometime later a group of wealthy, foreign dignitaries, who had followed a star to find the child, also sought out the family to bring them valuable gifts. They desired to honour and pay tribute to him—a gesture that foretold his stature as a king.

Following this visit, another angel appeared in a dream, instructing the young man to take his family to a distant country for their safety. Without hesitation, the family fled their native land.

The reigning king in their homeland had learned from the foreign dignitaries that a king had been born. Consumed with fear that his rule might be threatened, he unleashed a horrific genocide in the area, ordering every baby boy aged two and under to be slaughtered.

Once this paranoid, narcissistic leader died, the young man had another angelic encounter in a dream, assuring him that it was now safe to return to their country of origin.

The family lived a fulfilling life among their own people. The husband worked as a carpenter, and the family grew and thrived. However the parents fully recognised that their eldest son was no ordinary child.

While the boy learned his father's trade, as was the custom of the day, he also developed a deep understanding concerning issues of life based on his studies of the holy book of his people. The book communicated not only intellectual and relational knowledge, but also imparted spiritual insight that was very important within the boy's culture.

At an early age, the boy displayed wisdom well beyond his years and soon was engaging adults in deep spiritual discussions with knowledge and understanding superior to that of his elders.

Little more is known about this young man's life until he turned thirty years old. At that time he began speaking publicly to those who would listen, teaching them a better way of life called "The Way of Love," a simple life filled with purpose, meaning, and hope.

This young man's teachings were highly unconventional in religious circles of the time, yet they were refreshing and uplifting to the common people. His following grew, as did the crowd that gathered to hear him. Before long, his followers swelled to the thousands.

Those who surrounded him were often social outcasts or individuals marginalised by poverty, gender, nationality, infirmity, or untreatable diseases. While the religious leaders listened from the sidelines and scoffed at his message, his followers adored him and eagerly absorbed every word he spoke.

This young man made life remarkable. The extraordinary was ordinary around him. He healed people from any disease, affliction, and infirmity regardless of severity.

"Who is he?" people wondered. "He even takes authority over storms and calms raging seas." Among other wonders, he fed thousands with one child's lunch, raised people from the dead and cast demons out of others.

People were captivated by his teachings and ministry. He radiated compassion and love, in stark contrast to the religious elite they knew. Always giving and expecting nothing in return, he was authentic, and his love was genuine. He saw into their hearts and minds, valuing them for who they truly were. He understood their pain and struggles, speaking peace into their lives and offered hope in the darkest of circumstances.

It seemed impossible, but trouble was brewing. As the young man continued to challenge the religious elite about their self-serving behaviour, their fear and hatred of him grew in direct proportion to his rising popularity with the masses.

His fearless exposure of their agenda led him to confront them by saying, "You are like white-washed tombs, beautifully adorned on the outside, but inside you are filled with the putrid stench of decay and death."

This infuriated them, as they saw their power and control, built on rules and mandates, slipping away. They despised his disruptive teachings, which exposed their tyranny, hypocrisy, and abuse of power, revealing their deceitfulness for all to see.

His boldness and teachings were so radical. He urged everyone to love their enemies and pray for their persecutors—who had heard of such a thing?

His instructions on caring for widows, orphans, and the disadvantaged were extreme. "Give away your second coat if you own two," he said, "and in the same way share your food."

He became intolerable to the duplicitous spiritual leaders when they saw him offer people abundant life based on faith in himself and God's love, as opposed to the bondage their religious rules and regulations imposed.

The enraged religious leaders, sensing a decline in the power they held over the masses, devised a plan to eliminate him. They bribed one of his followers to betray him by falsely accusing him of plotting treason against governmental authorities. They incited crowds with misinformation and lobbied the regional governor, applying intense pressure to persuade him to adopt their unjust plans.

In a hysteria-fuelled frenzy, they swiftly and unjustly tried, convicted, and executed the young man at the age of thirty-three.

His heartbroken mother and a few close followers retrieved his body and gave him a quiet, dignified burial in a friend's tomb. They mourned deeply the tragic injustice, questioning why he had been so cruelly brutalised. This young man had loved so profoundly that even in the midst of his execution he asked God to have mercy on his murderers, saying, "Forgive them, for they know not what they do."

The young man's followers, confused and overwhelmed with grief, realised they could suffer a similar fate and went into hiding. A few days after his death, however, something extraordinary happened.

Early one morning, while it was dark, a woman who had dearly loved the young man arrived with flowers and spices at the burial site. The stone in front of his tomb had been rolled away, and the tomb was wide open. How could that be? She stooped to look inside. His body was gone, but two men in dazzling white robes stood where his body had been.

She panicked, wondering *Where is he? Who has stolen his body?* Tears of bewilderment and fear ran down her face.

"Why are you weeping?" asked a man standing outside the tomb, whom she thought was the gardener.

"They have taken his body, and I don't know where they have laid him!"

"He is not here; he is risen," he replied,

"If you have taken him, tell me where you have laid him so I can care for him," she pleaded.

"My friend," he said, his words filled with compassion.

Suddenly, she realised she was speaking to the very one she had come to honour.

"Teacher!" she breathed.

He responded, "Go to the others and tell them you have seen me."

The woman, overcome with astonishment and joy, ran to tell her friends that their beloved leader was alive.

The news quickly reached the political and religious leaders, and bedlam ensued. They frantically sought to find the body and bring an end to the narrative that he had risen from the dead. In desperation they labelled it as "total nonsense."

Things became even more bizarre when the young man suddenly appeared in various places, at unusual times, and to different people.

He joined some of his followers as they walked from one town to another, conversing with them along the way. It was only at the end of the journey that the men realised the identity of their fellow traveller.

On another occasion, he mysteriously appeared in a locked room where some of his believers were hiding from the religious leaders.

He even prepared a fish cookout for a group of his followers by the lake where they were fishing.

In another instance, more than five hundred people reported seeing him at the same time.

Each time, he spoke words of wisdom and comfort to his listeners, offering them the blessing of his peace through faith and trust in him.

These supernatural encounters helped the young man's followers understand his teachings more clearly. During his lifetime, they hadn't made sense of some of his instructions, especially those surrounding his death and resurrection. Later they remembered that he had said, "Listen to me very closely, because I am going away, and you will not see me again. In fact, I have to leave you so I can send you a special friend—someone who is a comforter, who will indwell you, teach you what you need to know, and guide you in all truth. He will help you fully understand what I have taught you, so you in turn can go into the world and teach others 'The Way of Love.' "

He urged them not to be anxious or fearful concerning anything and said, "I'm going ahead to prepare a place for you in Heaven. When you get there, I'll greet you with wide open arms and welcome you home. It is even better than what you can imagine or dream. All you have to do is believe in me." A small child quietly asked, "But who are you, Lord?"

He replied "My name is Yeshua, which is Isa in Arabic and Jesus in English."

This story of radical love remains as fresh and relevant today as it was when Jesus walked the earth. It brought Gerda and me to our most crucial crossroads in life.

CHAPTER 29

Crossroads

Life is full of adventures, mysteries, and turns. Many are exciting and planned, while others are totally unexpected and disconcerting. For me the process of writing this book falls into the latter category. Since I knew it was God's idea, not mine, I trusted him to provide the people, resources, and ideas to complete it. This was a huge crossroads in life that became a God-adventure for me.

Each one of us stands regularly at a crossroad where we have to make decisions that affect our future and the future of those around us. We ask ourselves, "*Should I take this road, or that one?*" Most are minor decisions, while others are life-altering. Some come in the natural progression of life, while others are sadly forced upon us.

Regardless of the magnitude of the decision, or what brought us to this intersection, we want to take the right and best way, the one that gives us the greatest joy, success, safety, fulfilment, and inner peace.

Sometimes an answer is hard to come by, or is confusing to figure out. At times the road we choose brings us to outcomes that are anything but wonderful. The good news is, there is always an opportunity to find the path that leads to the most precious gift of all—rest for our souls.

In the journey of life, many obstacles seek to block us from reaching the destiny of knowing God and his love. No matter how difficult things appear, as Frances Schaeffer said, "God is there. He is not silent, but rather he has made himself known to us in space, in time, and in history."

My hope and prayer is that we all choose the road that seeks God and asks him to reveal himself in some special way. Whether we are seasoned travellers, or first-time wanderers, we need his supernatural revelation to guide us.

We are all made in the image of God. He loves each of us and longs for us to have rest for our souls.

Even at death, Gerda had a profound sense of peace and rest in her soul because she knew her life wasn't over, but would continue in a place called Heaven.

As C.S. Lewis so aptly described life in Heaven when he wrote: "The Great Story, which no one on Earth has read and which goes on forever…in which every chapter is better than the one before." We get a glimpse into this epic story in the Book of Revelation that describes Heaven as The New Jerusalem:

"The dwelling place of God is with men. He will dwell with them, and they shall be his people, and God himself will be with them; he will wipe away every tear from their eyes, and death shall be no more, neither shall there be mourning, nor crying, nor pain anymore, for the former things have passed away." (Revelation 21:3–4, RSV*)*

No two travellers have walked the same road in life. We each have a unique life's journey, much of it determined by our choices, or the choices others make for us. God is inviting us to *choose life* and live life his way. He has a plan for our lives for good, to give us hope and a future. He wants us to experience his love and be at rest. Jesus said, *"Behold, I stand at the door and knock; if anyone hears my voice and opens the door, I will come in to him and eat with him, and he with me"* (Revelation 3:20, *RSV*). He enables us to discover the best possible story for our lives—one he has written for us.

The beauty of this news is that no one is holding us for ransom or twisting our arms to adopt a certain viewpoint. We all have free will to choose whether to open the door or not. We are invited to come as we are with all our fears, questions, and doubts. God isn't stumped by any of them and is inviting us to let him sit at our table to find answers and receive rest for our souls.

Questions don't oppose faith. They often lead to revelation and deeper understanding. Gerda was full of questions. She couldn't accept answers that didn't offer full explanations. As a result, she grew in faith. From her new vantage point in Heaven, I am convinced she is urging us, even more fervently than ever, to give God a chance.

Ask him if he is real. Ask him to reveal himself and his love to you. If you do, you will embark on the most exhilarating adventure you can possibly imagine.

Our family continues to grow, holding the memory of Gerda close in our hearts.

I loved you then,
I love you still.
I always have,
I always will.

NEW BEGINNINGS

Resources and Ministries

This is a selection of resources and ministries that helped Gerda and me grow in our intimacy with God. I trust some of them will help you in your adventure along this path.

The Bible

The Bible is the most important book ever published, and there is a very good reason why every year it is the world's best seller. I love the truth in an acrostic my good friend Norm Cheng uses for the word B.I.B.L.E. He says it stands for

Basic
Instruction
Before
Leaving
Earth

Gerda and I couldn't have agreed more, and that is why we bought each other a new Bible for our last Christmas together. We did it without knowing what we had planned to give each other.

In the Bible Gerda gave me, she wrote what is now one of my very precious notes from her:

"My dear Ian:

The year ahead is very uncertain. It looks like it could be our most challenging one. I wanted you to have something special from me this year and could think of nothing more valuable than God's Word. Hence this Bible.

How God's Word has helped us, sustained us, convicted us, comforted us, encouraged and inspired us as we journeyed through this life together!

How we have held onto the promises God gave us!

What would we ever have done without it, and without Jesus?

I pray that God will speak profoundly and powerfully to you through his Word."

If you are unfamiliar with the Bible, I recommend you start in the New Testament with the Books of Matthew, Mark, Luke, and John. They tell the story of the life of Jesus. The Book of John explains customs and meanings that people like me, without a Jewish background, may not otherwise understand.

You Version Bible App youversion.com

Gerda and I downloaded the You Version Bible App onto our smartphones. It was created by Bobby Gruenewald of Life Church. It is a free app that has been downloaded more than 850 million times in over 2,000 languages. The app gives access to biblically centred, relevant information and teaching that encourages and helps people seek God. Translated into many languages, it is the easiest and cheapest way to get a copy of God's Word while receiving many good biblical teaching resources. I recommend a modern translation of the Bible, such as *New International Version*, *English Standard Version*, or *The Message*, which is a paraphrased version of the Bible written in conversational English.

Bondage Breaker and *Victory Over the Darkness* by Neil Anderson ficm.org

Neil Anderson, a former aerospace engineer, wrote these two bestselling books to help people understand that through Christ, the "chains" that often bind us to harmful habits and irrational thinking can be broken. Early in our marriage, Gerda and I attended one of Neil's conferences and were greatly helped in building a firmer foundation for life through release from emotional and spiritual bondage.

Ellel Ministries global.ellel.org

Ellel Ministries, founded by Peter Horrobin, has as its foundational Scripture Luke 9.11: "*When the crowds learned it, they followed him, and he welcomed them and spoke to them of the Kingdom of God and cured those who had need of healing.*" Jesus *welcomed* the people, *taught* them about the Kingdom, and *healed* them. These three elements constitute the work of Ellel Ministries. More than fifty Ellel centres in at least thirty-five countries provide training and teaching to help people receive spiritual, emotional, and physical healing. These centres have many in-person and online courses to help individuals and couples receive freedom in Christ.

Don Dickerman Ministries liberatedliving.info

The apostle Paul said in Ephesians 6:12, *"For our struggle is not against flesh and blood, but against the rulers, against the authorities, against the powers of this dark world and against spiritual forces of evil in the heavenly realms."*

Gerda and I were very conscious of this raging battle in the spirit realm and had some understanding of how to put on God's armour to fight the fight. Don's YouTube podcast interview with Isaiah Saldivar and Vlad Savchuk led me to a greater understanding of our authority in Jesus for healing and deliverance from demonic forces.

Combat Prayers to Crush the Enemy
by John Ramirez johnramirez.org

John was formerly a high-ranking Satanist before his dramatic conversion in 1999 when he died and experienced the torments of hell and miraculously came back to life. As a result, he fully understands the importance of standing strong through prayer with the authority we have in Jesus. These books give you prayers to fight against the spiritual forces of evil in dark places, break their strongholds, and bring God's blessings into your life.

***The Biggest Idea Ever* by Denis Beausejour**

denisbeausejour.com

This high-powered and hard-driving VP of marketing for Proctor & Gamble shares how he discovered the Kingdom of Heaven and traded anxiety, fear, and burnout for peace, purpose, and significance. Denis honestly and openly communicates his journey of transformation and how he subsequently left the security of his prestigious job to be undivided in helping others in the same life adventure.

***The Case for Christ* by Lee Strobel**

leestrobel.com

This book and film tell the true story of how Lee Strobel, a trained forensic journalist who worked for the *Chicago Tribune*, set out as an atheist to disprove the existence of God. He applied his training as a critically thinking journalist, travelled extensively, met with experts from many disciplines, and asked deep, penetrating questions. When he analysed and reviewed the information, he concluded that the Bible was true and turned from unbelief to faith.

***Evidence that Demands a Verdict* and *More than a Carpenter* by Josh McDowell josh.org**

Josh McDowell, originally another avid atheist, discovered compelling and overwhelming evidence for the reliability of the Christian faith. As a result, he wrote these books and many others to explain why he is now a believer. Some of the logical reasoning Lee Strobel and Josh McDowell unpack in these resources helped me realize that I would need more faith to believe God does not exist than to believe he does.

Alpha Course alpha.org

This course is available in more than one hundred countries worldwide. It offers an excellent opportunity to watch a thought-provoking film series, meet with other seekers, ask questions around a dinner table, and enjoy a free meal. Countless people, including many of our friends, understand more fully the personal application, importance, and relevance of Jesus's teachings because of this course.

The Navigators navigators.org
navigators.org/resource/the-bridge-to-life

The Navigators helped me understand Jesus's teachings and what it means to follow him and implement disciplines to help me nurture my relationship with God. Navigators' groups are found in many countries throughout the world. They provide many excellent Bible study materials and resources to help individuals know God and grow in their faith as disciples of Jesus.

***Experiencing God: Knowing and Doing the Will of God* by Henry and Richard Blackaby and Claude King blackaby.org**

This book, published in forty-seven languages with more than seven million copies in print, describes the way the authors understand and walk with God. The study has helped transform millions of people from all walks of life, from prisoners to presidents of countries. Gerda and I had the privilege of meeting the Blackaby family. We were deeply blessed by the practical and insightful teaching that challenged us to align our lives with God's agenda.

How Should We Then Live? by Francis Schaeffer labri.org

Francis Schaeffer and his writings were among Gerda's favourites, and she often referred to this book, now also a film.
At age seventeen, Schaeffer had a thirst for answers to life, especially after reading a book on Greek philosophy. He realised philosophers asked many questions, yet seemed to have no answers to the basic problems of the human condition. In 1955, he and his wife Edith opened their home in Switzerland to anyone who had questions concerning faith. This home was called L'Abri, which means shelter, a place where anyone is welcome to come for a period of time to wrestle through questions about God and the significance of life. There are a handful of L'Abri centres throughout the world. Most offer accommodations suitable for singles, although some locations can host families.

***Heaven is for Real* by Todd Burpo heavenlive.org**

This book and movie tell the astounding story about the author's son Colton, who, when he was three years and ten months old, was very close to death five days after a misdiagnosis of a ruptured appendix. While doctors desperately tried to save his life, Colton went to Heaven and returned to tell an amazing story about it. Gerda and I read the story soon after it was published and appreciate more than ever that Heaven is for real. This truth became even more precious to us during the last nine months of Gerda's life, and to me since then.

90 Minutes in Heaven by Don Piper

donpiperministries.com

This is another book and movie about someone who went to Heaven and returned. Don's experience in Heaven was so spectacular, he had to deal with depression after he returned because he didn't want to be back on Earth. This is the book from which Moira Brown read to Gerda only moments before she passed away. I believe those words were preparing her for paradise awaiting her only minutes later.

The Hiding Place by Corrie Ten Boom

This is the captivating story in book and movie format about the author referenced in the chapter "Tapestry."

Revealing the Mysteries of Heaven by

David Jeremiah davidjeremiah.org

David Jeremiah was one of Gerda's favourite Bible teachers. She loved his straightforward, deep, and thoughtful teaching and often listened to him on the radio or TV. One of his series, "Revealing the Mysteries of Heaven," helped answer questions about what he termed "the happiest location in the universe."

Beth Moore lproof.org

Beth Moore was probably my wife's all-time favourite Bible teacher. She loved Beth's passion for seeking deep truth from God's Word and unapologetically applying it to everyday life. Living Proof Ministries, which Beth founded, has helped millions of women grow in their relationship with God. Beth's in-depth, practical teaching, which included her own struggles, failings, and life challenges, such as her journey of healing from childhood sexual abuse, had a profound impact on Gerda. A huge shout-out to Beth for being a special mentor, friend, and teacher to my sweetheart, even though they never met in person.

Beth inspired Gerda to pursue her passion to "be an illuminator of God's Word," especially through our church's Tuesday morning Bible study.

Above all, Beth, thank you for inspiring Gerda to write the letter to Jesus that I found—now a treasured keepsake—and referenced in the chapter, "A Time to Dance."

***Sensible Shoes* by Sharon Garlough Brown**

sharongarloughbrown.com

This was one of Gerda's favourite book series. *Sensible Shoes* is the story of four women who didn't know each other before attending the same retreat. Through their shared experiences, they embarked on a journey together, embracing spiritual practices that deepened their personal relationship with God. Along the way they moved from brokenness to wholeness, emerging from isolation and various struggles into a profound rest of heart and soul.

Gerda was so eager to meet Sharon, the author, at the Wesley Acres retreat in July 2018. It was there that Sharon candidly shared her story about her struggle to believe in God's love. Her testimony helped Gerda see God's love more clearly—beautifully through the colour yellow. Sharon, you are the reason this story exists. Thank you! Words cannot fully express our gratitude. One day, I hope to meet you and give you a hug on behalf of Gerda, myself and family, to thank you for being the catalyst that helped us recognise the wonder of God's love more clearly.

Compass Point Bible Church compasspointbc.com

Compass Point Bible Church (formerly Park Bible Church and Brant Bible Church) has been our home church since we married in 1981. It was also Gerda's church four years prior to that. It always was a very important cornerstone in our lives and provided a caring community of people who turned up "big time," especially during Gerda's illness. We wouldn't have wanted to do life without them.

Muskoka Bible Centre muskokabible.com

This 230-acre campground/conference centre located on Mary Lake, just south of Huntsville, was our favourite family summer destination. We spent many vacations enjoying the beautiful outdoor life Muskoka offers, as well as the inspirational teachings of many gifted Bible teachers. Our times there always provided great refreshment of spirit, soul, and body. The centre is now a favourite summer destination for my children, who now take their children there.

Lauren Daigle laurendaigle.com

Music is a pathway to the soul and reaches the innermost parts of our beings. It strengthened and quieted us during the challenging times of Gerda's illness. We thrived on it. Gerda filled our home with worship music, and I searched YouTube on my early morning walks looking for comfort through my tears. Cat Stevens' rendition of "Morning Has Broken" became a daily staple, the lyrics fortifying me as I sang along to the chorus:

Morning has broken, like the first morning.
Blackbird has spoken, like the first bird.
Praise for the singing, praise for the morning,
Praise for them springing fresh from the world.

During these walks providentially I stumbled upon Lauren Daigle whose smoky, alto voice quickly drew me. Many of her meaningful lyrics became the cry of my heart, resonating powerfully into the depth of my being like some of these from "You Alone," "Peace Be Still," and "Carry On"

When life has overwhelmed me
And I feel like giving up
I cling to all You've promised
It will always be enough

When the world around me crumbles
And it's hard to understand
I will run to You, my shelter
I am safe within Your hands
Oh, You are my helper forever

I will not fear
God, you are with me
I know You're near
You'll never leave me
I will trust in You alone

When I'm broken in the silence
I can hear you whispering,
"You're not alone here in these trials
I would hold you faithfully"
Oh, you are my help forever

Peace be still
Say the word and I will
Set my feet upon the sea
Till I'm dancing in the deep;
Oh peace be still!
You are here, so it is well.
Even when my eyes can't see
I will trust the voice that speaks
Peace, peace over me.

I know it hurts!
It's hard to breathe sometimes.
These nights are long;
You've lost the will to fight.
Is anybody out there?
Can you lead me to the light?
Is anybody out there?
Tell me it'll all be alright.
You are not alone;
I've been here the whole time
Singing you a song.
I will carry you.
I will carry you.

Lauren has many original recordings filled with meaningful and powerful words. I could write a book about them, including the duets she sings with Jon Foreman, lead singer of Switchfoot, called "I Won't Let You Go" and "A Place Called Earth."

The Sacred Romance by Brent Curtis and John Eldridge wildatheart.org

John Eldridge wrote the bestselling book *Wild at Heart* about discovering the secret of a man's soul. In *The Sacred Romance*, he and Brent Curtis unpack how one draws closer to God even in hurt, disappointment, and evil in life.

Love Does by Bob Goff lovedoes.org

Bob Goff describes himself as a "recovering lawyer." He lives life in permanent overdrive and will go to any length to love others, as revealed in his book *Love Does*. He used the profits from the sale of this book to help disadvantaged people, especially children, by providing schooling opportunities they would otherwise not have had. These schools are located in areas of severe conflict around the world: Uganda, India, Nepal, Iraq, Somalia, Afghanistan, and the Democratic Republic of Congo. Bob even opened a school for witch doctors in Uganda. He tells this story in his second book, *Everybody, Always*. He really does *Dream Big*—the title of his third book.

Thank you, Bob Goff, for being such a wonderful and crazy lover of people. What an awe-inspiring difference you are making in this world! Thank you also "Sweet Maria," Bob's adorable wife who kept the home fires burning and lights on while he embarked on many of his audacious adventures. What a privilege it has been to meet you both! Had Gerda met you, she would have loved you as much as I do.

Grief Share griefshare.org

This is a grief recovery and support program designed to help individuals navigate the grieving process. The GriefShare program is available in over thirty countries and is often led by people who have personally experienced significant loss.

Others

It's so important for us to find people who will help and encourage us to grow in knowing God. Sadly, sometimes it is necessary to go outside our current community to find those who will stand non-judgmentally with us, love us, and only seek our best interests.

Prayer Available 24/7; billygraham.org and crossroads.ca

You are not alone. Prayer is central to every religion because it is the heart of man seeking the heart of God. If you would like prayer for yourself regarding any situation call anytime toll free 1-855-255-7729 Billy Graham Evangelistic Organisation or 1-866-273-4441 Crossroads Christian Communications. Both ministries were founded on prayer and their goal is to ensure everyone has the opportunity to pray with someone.

The Bridge to Life

Both Gerda and I, at different points in our lives, realised there was a separation between ourselves and God. When I was nineteen I didn't know, or particularly care, if he existed, but for Gerda it was different. She knew from an early age that God was there. She just lacked understanding of what she needed to do to step into a right relationship with him.

As we individually walked the path of life we came to discover that Jesus, by dying on the cross for our sins, bridged the chasm separating us from a holy God. Faith in Jesus allowed us to come as we were and cross that divide into a living relationship with God. He accepted us with all our questions, doubts, burdens, and imperfections. These are Jesus' promises to everyone:

> Come to me, all who are weary and burdened, and I will give you rest. Take my yoke upon you and learn from me, for I am gentle and humble in heart, and you will find rest for your souls. For my yoke is easy and my burden is light.
> *(Matthew 11:28-30,* NIV*)*

> For God so loved the world that he gave his only begotten Son, that whoever believes in him shall not perish but have eternal life. For God did not send his Son into the world to condemn the world, but to save the world through him.
> *(John 3:16-17,* NIV*)*

> Truly, truly I say to you, he who hears my word and believes him who sent me has eternal life. He does not come into judgement but has passed from death to life.
> *(John 5:24,* NIV*)*

> I am the bread of life, whoever comes to me will never go hungry, and whoever believes in me will never thirst.
> *(John 6:35,* NIV*)*

I have come that they may have life and have it to the full.
I am the good shepherd. The good shepherd lays down his
life for his sheep.
(John 10:10b–11, NIV*)*

As we grew in our understanding of who Jesus is, and his purpose on Earth, both Gerda and I individually took the opportunity to believe in him. We crossed the bridge from doing life our way to doing it God's way, which is often referred to as the "Bridge to Life." Steps to making this crossing are as simple as A B C C

Acknowledge God exists.
Believe Jesus is who he claimed to be.
Confess you are a sinner and Jesus died for your sin.
Commit to living life God's way.

This is the place of total surrender where God will walk with us in every situation in which we find ourselves. It is a place of transformation where we come exactly the way we are, with all our imperfections and failures, humbly seeking his forgiveness for all we have done wrong. And then we receive his healing touch.

This journey toward an intimate relationship with God is definitely the most epic and fulfilling adventure Gerda and I ever embarked upon.

For me, it started when I was twenty years old with a simple prayer: "Yes God, I believe. Take me, break me, and remake me!"

These were the first stumbling words I spoke to God as I chose to cross the Bridge to Life. Since then I have prayed many more prayers as I continued pressing on to know him.

What On Earth Am I Doing On Earth?

I asked myself that question in my early forties. I wasn't depressed or despondent. Life was very good, especially at that point. My marriage and family life had been rekindled. However, I felt there was more to life than what I was experiencing. At that time, I read two books that helped crystallise and confirm some of my thinking.

The Purpose Driven Life, by Rick Warren, and *HalfTime* by Bob Buford.

Rick Warren's book, with more than fifty million copies worldwide and translated into one hundred and thirty-five languages, asks a similar question to the one I was pondering: "What on Earth am I here for?" He starts the book by writing, "It's not about you," and explains God's five purposes for us:

1. You were planned for God's pleasure.
2. You were formed for God's family.
3. You were created to become like Christ.
4. You were shaped to serve God.
5. You were created for a mission.

Buford's book explores how, in the first half of our lives, we focus on success—pursuing an education, finding a life partner, and establishing our careers and families. In the second half of our life, our focus shifts to seeking significance as we strive to create a legacy greater than ourselves, one that will endure beyond our time on Earth.

Gerda shared this same heartbeat with me, and during the last twenty-five years of our marriage, we experienced some exciting times in our pursuit for more significance. This pursuit included working alongside Debbie Moir-Tigchelaar, Ross and Linda Drummond, and others in establishing Drummond House in Waterdown, just outside of Burlington, a transition home for women and children needing a temporary safe haven while rebuilding their lives and healing from various life traumas. In 2007, I was part of a task force that organised a series of national conferences entitled "Purpose@Work" where people were challenged on how to integrate their faith into the workplace and have a greater purpose than simply making a profit. For fifteen years, until 2023, a group of us pursued this vision through a local Burlington/Oakville group called Christ in the Workplace that met monthly. Gerda was given the opportunity to fulfill a greater purpose when Amy Dempsey recognised her teaching ability and invited her to teach the Bible at our church and in various communities in Ontario through Pioneer Camp Ministries. Gerda was always energised by the opportunity to illuminate practical and relevant truths from Scripture; it truly was her "sweet spot," where she thrived.

Now we have another purpose: the sharing of *Yellow a love story.*

YellowALoveStory.com

YellowALoveStory.com exists to tell the story of God's love, and how he sometimes reveals it to us in mysterious ways, especially during dark times in our lives. Profits from the sale of this book are directed to fulfil the purpose of telling this story and supporting others with a similar vision.

If you are interested in helping share this story anywhere in the world, you are invited to contact us.

For additional copies of this book, or for information on how to become a distributor, or for creative fundraising ideas for your favourite charity, please contact: info@ YellowALoveStory.com

AFTERWORD

The days, weeks, months, and years are slipping by since we received my wife's diagnosis that turned our world upside down. The loving community of people surrounding me often ask how I am doing. My answer is mixed, depending on what time of year it is and whether it is around any significant date or anniversary.

One thing is for certain: time brings healing, with the paradox of grief and joy existing side by side, like a set of railroad tracks. One moment I find myself on the track of grief, the next on the track of joy. The most important thing I've learned is not to get stuck on just one track—often easier said than done.

Many times grief brings darkness that results in profound hopelessness not unlike what Jesus' followers experienced at the end of his life on Earth. Darkness covered Earth at that time to try and snuff out his message of hope, love, and faith.

In the Garden of Gethsemane where olives are grown and pressed, Jesus was betrayed by one of his closest friends, someone whom he loved dearly and with whom he shared the intimacy of life. Through treachery he was unjustly condemned to a barbaric, humiliating death, mercilessly lashed, beaten, and nailed to a cross at Golgotha, ensuring his last few hours were filled only with excruciating agony. Even the heavens screamed against such wickedness, and darkness covered the land.

Darkness continually seeks to invade our lives bringing despair, defeat, and a feeling of hopelessness. It finds us through difficult and devastating situations, often very unfair and so many times outright evil. In my times of walking in the garden of grief with darkness seemingly around every corner trying to consume me, I have discovered many treasures. These "treasures in darkness" are not necessarily new discoveries, but are revelations, or realisations that have become cemented in my soul as never before through concepts such as Heaven is real, and God loves me.

God spoke these words through the prophet Isaiah: "… *since you are precious and honoured in my sight and I love you*" (Isaiah 43:4, *NIV*). I remember the day I read this Scripture for the first time. It seemed like God was with me in the room, saying in an audible voice, I*an, I love you!* I had never heard these words spoken to me by anyone before. I knew I was loved by my family and others, but for the first time in my life, as a twenty-one-year-old, I was actually hearing the words, *Ian, I love you!* and it was God himself speaking to me. The impact was profound. I can still hear those words today. Throughout Gerda's illness, we continually saw God's goodness and love revealed to us.

Through the prophet Jeremiah, God also said, *"I have loved you with an everlasting love; I have drawn you with unfailing kindness"*

(Jeremiah 31:3, *NIV*).

Such radical, unfailing love lasts forever. That's the story of God's love—the real love story.

God's heart is for us. The number one purpose in life is to let God love us. If we allow him to do this, we will experience his goodness and mercy, as he clearly says:

The Lord is my Shepherd; I shall not want. He makes me lie down in green pastures. He leads me beside still waters. He restores my soul. He leads me in paths of righteousness for his name's sake. Even though I walk through the valley of the shadow of death, I will fear no evil, for you are with me. Your rod and staff comfort me. You prepare a table before me in the presence of my enemies. You anoint my head with oil; my cup overflows. Surely goodness and mercy shall follow me all the days of my life, and I shall dwell in the house of the Lord forever. *(Psalm 23,* ESV*)*

Not only is God continuing to pursue me with his love, but many of my family and friends are cheering me along in unique and special ways. One of these came in the form of a

"Hug from Heaven" I received about six months after Gerda passed away.

One day when I returned home and went into my bedroom, I was shocked to see a beautiful new bedspread on my bed. It was yellow, with embroidered yellow roses and a light blue border. In its centre was a large oval with similar edging surrounding a large rose on a yellow background. On top of the bedspread was a letter.

My Dearest Ian:

I've been thinking about you so much these past few months.

I have missed you so much…. I don't even know where to begin to tell you how wonderful Heaven is. It is nothing short of amazing. You would love it!

I am having the time of my life. Matthew is the most wonderful child. He brings me so much joy, and I can't wait for you to meet him. He's mischievous and has a special sparkle in his eyes just like you, Love.

I wish you were here with me. I have had many conversations with Jesus, as to when you can come be with me. Jesus assures me that the time has not yet come for you to join us up here. He tells me you have some very important work to do. You are the man he needs to tell the world about the love story he has given us.

Oh Ian! God is so good…. You are the perfect pick to write the story.

I have a beautiful window in Heaven [where] I look down and see all my loved ones.

Love, I'm so proud you are listening and obeying God's call on your life.

I see how all your grandchildren are loving having you around. Give them extra hugs and love for me. And please don't forget to remind them how much I love them: so, so much!

Did you know, sometimes God allows me to come back and visit? God allowed me to be present at Suzie's house, and I was able to watch Clara being born! What an amazing job Suzie did! She's such a strong woman. And Clara Rose is perfect.

Speaking of new grandchildren: Oh Ian, can you believe it? We are expecting another grandchild! Oh that is so wonderful. I just know you are going to be such a great Grandad to all our current grandchildren and grandchildren to come in this next season of life.

I know being apart is hard. I wish it wasn't this way. I wish we could be together now. I hear every time you talk to me, and I wish so badly I could talk back with you. However, we have to trust God that this is the way it's supposed to be right now. So I tried to figure out how to send you an "I love you" gift from Heaven. I found the perfect gift. This bedspread is to remind you of Me and my Love for You and God and his Love for Us Both.

So my Dearest Ian, when you lay down and rest, may you feel my love beside you, may you feel God's love enveloped all around you, may you find the peace you need. May you get the rest you need at the end of each day, so that you can do the work God has planned ahead for you to do.

I love you Ian with all my heart and soul.

All my love,

Gerda

P.S. My daughter Liz orchestrated this heartwarming "Hug from Heaven" for me, and it means so much to me.

Thank you for journeying this path with us—a story woven with the mystery of God and the beauty of his love, which shone through the darkness, gently leading us to his heart through Jesus and inviting us all to delve deeper into his love.

DELVE DEEPER

Personal Study and Group Discussion Questions

After reviewing each chapter, ask: 'What event or concept in this chapter had the greatest impact on you, and why? Follow up your answer with the question below pertaining to the same chapter.

Prologue

Have you ever done anything outside your comfort zone, or normal routine? If so, what were the circumstances that led to that action?

Share something someone did or said that was truly special to you and how it made you feel?

Chapter 1: Gerda, My Sweetheart

Think of a time when you recalled a special memory of someone who is no longer with you. What images and emotions did that memory retrieve?

Chapter 2: Our Meeting

Share how you met someone who has played a very important role in your life.

Chapter 3: Special Attraction

Have any of your ancestors experienced difficult or dangerous situations? How did they handle them and how does this knowledge impact you?

Chapter 4: Beached

Have you told someone your deepest feelings for them, and they didn't respond the way you had hoped? If so what was your response?

Chapter 5: Reunion

Have you ever been certain of your direction only to learn that you made the wrong decision? How did you deal with it?

Chapter 6: Candid Words

Can you think of a situation when a hindrance proved to be a huge benefit?

Chapter 7: Will You Marry Me?

Is there a time when you persevered in the face of unfavourable circumstances? What was the outcome?

Chapter 8: The Wedding

Describe the most memorable experience from your wedding or someone else's. What made it so special?

Chapter 9: Family

Explain your immediate or extended family dynamics and what you appreciate most about your family members.

Chapter 10: Storm Clouds

Identify a difficult time in your life that you discovered you were partly or fully responsible for creating.

Chapter 11: Rebuilding

Have you had a broken relationship that was restored? How was it re-built and what was the outcome?

Chapter 12: God, Family, and Business

What does God mean to you, and what led you to that understanding?

Chapter 13: The Best Christmas Ever

Identify an annual celebration that's important to you. What significance does it hold for you and why?

Chapter 14: Yellow

Describe something that keeps recurring in your life. Why do you think it keeps recurring? Does it prompt you to think that someone may be watching over you?

Chapter 15: Next Steps

Have you ever been given significant advice? Whether you followed it or not, what impact did it have—or could have had—on your life?

Chapter 16: The Blessing

Has there been a difficult season in your life that you now see as a blessing? Reflect on it.

Chapter 17: The Valley of the Shadow of Death

Have you ever had an experience that made you think there is more to life than what your five senses indicate? How did that experience influence your beliefs?

Chapter 18: It's Time to Go

If you have experienced extraordinary or inexplicable circumstances surrounding someone's passing, share how they affected you.

Chapter 19: Farewell, My Beloved

Have you said a special goodbye to a loved one who was passing away? What words did you use?

Chapter 20: Celebration of Love: The Setting

Share a memory of a funeral service or Celebration of Life you attended that left you with an indelible positive memory.

Chapter 21: Celebration of Love: Matthew

Have you ever had a vision or a significant dream you believed carried a special message for you, or have you ever seen an angel or experienced something supernatural? If so, share how it affected you and made you feel?

Chapter 22: Celebration of Love: Gerda's Special Message

Is God's love real to you? Have you ever asked God to reveal himself or his love to you? If so what was the outcome?

Chapter 23: Celebration of Love: The Invitation

If you are carrying, or have carried, any weariness or heaviness, can you talk about it?

Chapter 24: "Hold my Hand; We Will Walk in the Sand"

What do you love doing with someone close to you, and why is it special to you?

Chapter 25: Tapestry

Share a difficult and/or painful experience that later gave you a foundation from which to help others in similar situations.

Chapter 26: Circles of Life

Can you identify and talk about any personal "circles of life" you have experienced?

Chapter 27: Time to Dance

What would you love to do most in life if there were no limitations based on finances, ability, or circumstances?

Chapter 28: Radical Love

Have you ever read (or heard) the life story of Jesus, and if so, how did it affect you?

Chapter 29: Crossroads

In your walk toward the heart of God, are you aware of something you need to do to get closer to him?

New Beginnings

God loves you deeply and is patiently knocking on the door of your heart, waiting for you to welcome him in. Is there anything holding you back from opening that door and inviting Jesus into your life? If not you may want to consider following the ABCC steps outlined in the Resource Section:

- Acknowledge God exists.
- Believe Jesus is who he claimed to be.
- Confess you are a sinner and Jesus died for your sin.
- Commit to living life God's way.

If we can do anything to support you in any way on this journey, don't hesitate to contact us at **yellowalovestory@gmail.com**

EPILOGUE

In my wildest dreams I never imagined authoring anything, let alone a book about love. I am an English real estate agent who became a Canadian REALTOR®. My life was turned upside down when cancer snatched the woman of my dreams from my arms.

This is my story of how I experienced the love of family, friends and God, especially during the dark time of losing my wife and coming to understand more fully how love conquers all. I trust this story encourages and blesses you in a practical way as you experience love and travel the road called *Life*.

The inspiration behind Yellow a love story

ABOUT THE AUTHOR

Ian W. McSporran was born in Northern England and spent his childhood on his parents' dairy farms in the picturesque Yorkshire Dales, growing up alongside his four siblings. The family later moved to the seaside town of Morecambe, known for its stunning views across the bay to the world-renowned Lake District.

In 1980, Ian emigrated to Canada to pursue the love of his life, Gerda, whom he married the following year. For 38 years, they made their home in Burlington, just west of Toronto on the shores of Lake Ontario. A life long REALTOR®, Ian continues to reside there and is grateful to have all three of his children and nine grandchildren nearby. He enjoys a full life—balancing time with family, friends, his trusted real estate team and clients, cheering on his childhood football team, Burnley, and remaining actively involved in his local church community.

Printed in Canada